Margaret Mann's book of personal essays, *A Dramatically Different Direction*, stands out as singularly unique. Her viewpoint and experience is valuable not only because she is different in so many ways, but also because she turns what might segregate her from the mainstream to an ingratiating asset – an indomitable spirit that teaches us to be content with our circumstances, whatever they might be.

Tim Gilmer, Editor, New Mobility Magazine

What a hoot! *A Dramatically Different Direction* is poignant and often funny commentary on disability. With a keen wit and well balanced mockery, Margaret Mann shares her unique perspective on living a real life in the aftermath of a serious disability.

Susan M. Daniels, former Deputy Director, Social Security Administration

Margaret Mann is the Buddha on the road in a wheelchair. Her memoir is the story of a wise and generous woman who embraces all that life deals her with gusto. She gives new meaning to mindfulness, new depth to compassion. The book, like the woman, is a jewel.

Mary Hunt, Co-Director of the Women's Alliance for Theology, Ethics and Ritual (W.A.T.E.R.), author of Fierce Tenderness: A Feminist Theology of Friendship

Being aware of the effort it takes to make profound thoughts compelling, and complicated experiences coherent and engaging, I especially appreciated *A Dramatically Different Direction*. Margaret Mann has written a wise and witty primer on both disability and the proper approach to life, and reading it has substantially furthered my education on both counts. If everyone read this book, everyone's life would be better.

Alix Dobkin, Singer, Songwriter, Author of My Red Blood: A Memoir of Growing Up Communist, Coming Onto the Greenwich Village Folk Scene, and Coming Out in the Feminist Movement.

Margaret Mann is a passionate lover of life with a fabulous wit. I think of her advice everyday of my life. Her story will amaze you.

Barbara Higbie, Singer, Songwriter

A Dramatically Different Direction

Margaret Mann

ISBN: 1463660650

ISBN-13: 9781463660659

Library of Congress Control Number: 2011911173

CreateSpace, North Charleston, SC

To Margaret Brown (1940–2011),
my good friend, who died
before she got to read this book

Contents

Acknowledgments

This project began with Cathy Cade, Personal Historian, encouraging me to write my life story. I will be forever grateful for her encouragement. I am grateful to Ann Brown and Ruthann Ross for their willingness to read and reread my manuscript. I am grateful to the Church of the Crossroads Writer's Group for listening to and commenting on the many chapters under development. I am grateful to Monica Staub, Brigitte Savage, Stan Bliss, Judith Treesberg, Monique Bilezikian, Meade Andrews, and Melva Ware for their friendship through this entire ordeal. I am grateful to Leanne Logan and Susan Lucas for their wise counseling. I am grateful to Barbara Higbie for being my musical muse. I am grateful to the Pohulani Ladies Sewing Circle and Terrorist Society for providing piña coladas on the lanai during the tsunami alerts. I am grateful for my friend Jane Noe and her husband, Dennis, for their support of me all these years. I am grateful for Arvillie Anon for massaging this tired old body with amazing skill and spirit. And finally I am grateful to my niece, Jennifer; my brother, Chris; my first sister-in-law, Nalani; her husband, Rob; and my nephew, David; for providing me with the family I dreamed about.

Introduction

On March 1, 1997, when I was fifty-two years old, I went out to dinner with friends. Four months later I returned home in a wheelchair. A blood vessel had burst inside my spinal cord, leaving me instantly paralyzed from the waist down. I now use a wheelchair full time.

In the years since, that blood vessel has taken my mind, body, and spirit on a journey I could not have imagined in my wildest dreams. In a split second, my life took off in a dramatically different direction than I thought it was headed. When my life turned upside down, I was forced to learn how to make sense of senseless random events and to learn how to rebuild a satisfying life. I was forced to learn what it is like to be disabled, how to circumvent hostile environments, and how to endure ridiculous government policies.

My coping skills were forged in a multicultural crucible. I am a Caucasian/Apache woman raised in Hawai'i by a Zen Buddhist. I am also a lifelong lesbian with a passion for civil rights. Before the burst blood vessel, I had a long career as a community organizer working in the national offices of women's organizations in Washington, DC. The inspiration for my recovery has come from my Buddhist practice and also from author Byron Katie in *A Thousand Names for Joy*; both have taught me that you will suffer in life to the same degree you wish things were different. . I could wish that I were not in pain 24-7, or that I could once again walk along the beach and feel the water wash over my feet. I could wish that my income had not been cut in half. I could wish that I was still independent, living and working where I pleased. I could wish all these things and suffer magnificently…but I choose not to.

Everything about my disability has been a lesson in how nothing stays the same (the Buddhist notion of impermanence). At age fifty-two, I thought I was at the height of my career and would continue to earn a good income until I retired some years in the future. But you never know.

It also became clear to me since my life was altered by that little blood vessel that there really is no inherent value to any given experience. Is it better to be able-bodied or disabled? I know now that we simply get to choose how we will feel about everything that happens. You could choose to think your life is ruined by being paralyzed and suffer marvelously…or you could think of it, as I do, as a fascinating turn of events that teaches you something new every minute. You get to choose. By letting go of the story of what was and embracing what is, you won't suffer quite as much. It was a hard lesson to learn, but I think I finally got it.

Years later, I have rebuilt my life. Most days my pain is just an interesting sensation calling me to be present. I now feel strong and independent rolling along in my wheelchair. I like going fast down the sidewalk in my electric scooter and showing off a bit. Finding a way to make a living through a maze of obstructive government regulations is an interesting challenge. I have always been an idea-a-minute-person, and my disability has presented me with dozens of challenges each day. How will I get the wheelchair in the Miata? How will I get myself and my wheelchair up a long flight of stairs? How am I going to get the box of corn flakes off the top shelf in the supermarket? I have to think, plan, and scheme constantly. It keeps the juices flowing.

But there is more to me than my disability. I have family and friends and appealing things to do each day. Until recently, I was the chair of the board for the local LGBT (lesbian, gay, bisexual, and transgendered) community center. I earn my living through a counseling practice. I organize monthly dinners and a book club for the lesbian community on Oahu. I participate in a 'writers' group and have had articles published in national magazines. I attend weekly meditation sittings when I can. I am in training to become a docent at the Honolulu Academy of Arts. I swim three days a week. I live alone, and I get out daily on my scooter to go to lunch with friends or run errands. I try to start off the day by meditating quietly on my lanai, twenty-five floors up, overlooking beautiful Honolulu and the harbor. A rainbow often appears stretched out across the city. I enjoy life and actually find most of it very funny and filled with moments of astonishing grace.

But I am no saint. I melt down occasionally, overwhelmed by it all. Some days I wake up wishing I had died in the night. On occasion I yell at a driver who didn't see me in a crosswalk. I have raked a restaurant manager or two over the coals for failing to provide an accessible bathroom. I don't walk on water, and I am no Pollyanna who sees the silver lining behind every dark cloud. I can get worked up about the lack of ramps, or government regulations on income, and so forth. But I am an old, biracial, lesbian Buddhist in a wheelchair who refuses to suffer by sitting around wishing things were different.

Chapter 1

The Beginning: Demons from Hell

It started after dinner with a little buzz in my left leg. Within seconds I was shrieking at the top of my lungs. Demons from hell had taken hold of my lower abdomen and were ripping the flesh right off my bones. It was a most excruciating, unbelievable pain. And it came out of nowhere. I was sitting on the couch talking to a friend and *Slam! Bam!* I was screaming my head off.

I am not a screamer. I am not given to dramatic demonstrations. When I cut my finger I might say, "Oh darn!" When I got the news my mother died, a few tears leaked out, but that was all. But that night I made up for lost time. A few minutes after the onset, the pain subsided slightly, and I finally stopped screaming. We were shocked to discover that I could not move my legs…or feel them. I poked them several times to see if I could make any meaning of it all. How could this happen? Nothing made sense. I didn't know what to think.

Luckily there was a hospital just three blocks away. My friend, cool as a cucumber, knocked on her neighbor's door and asked him to help carry me to the car. They carried me down a flight of stairs and across the lawn to the car in a kitchen chair, pausing every few feet to rest. The fog in my brain was lifting, and a weird detached, problem-solving mode took its place. My legs were falling all over the place as they tried to get me into the car. We finally figured out to thread me like a needle and pull me backward from the opposite side into the car. Off we went to Washington Adventist Hospital in Takoma Park, Maryland. I learned later the pain was caused by a cramped iliopsoas muscle. It is a short, thick muscle that originates on the front of the spinal column, passes under the intestines, and attaches on the thigh bone to move the legs. It remained very painful for nearly a year.

The doctors at Washington Adventist took an X-ray and decided they could not help me. I felt like this was happening to someone else. This could have been a nightmare or TV program for all I knew. I thought I was very calm, but then I threw up. Some part of me realized that we were in *deep kimchi,* as we say in Hawaii, but my frontal lobes were in firm denial. After an hour or so they loaded me into an ambulance bound for Georgetown University Hospital in Washington, DC.

Lying on a gurney ready to be loaded into the ambulance, I heard my friend ask the ambulance driver how to get to Georgetown. "I don't know; I'm from Bowie, Maryland," he responded.

The part of my brain in firm denial spoke up from the gurney and I directed him: "Go down Carroll Avenue, and turn right...."They were incredulous that I was that alert, but little did they know that denial can go a long way. En route, from the back of the ambulance, I could see that we had made a wrong turn. "You were supposed to turn right back there!" I hollered. They made a U-turn, and off we went. All this helpfulness from one who laid there paralyzed from the waist down...and of course totally in touch with what was happening to her!

We arrived at Georgetown around midnight. God knows when we would have gotten there if I had left it to the good old boys to make their own way to the hospital! Once inside, they told my friend that she couldn't stay because she wasn't a family member. Turns out this was just the beginning of a very torturous isolation, as they did not let any of my friends in to see me until late the next day.

The whiz kids at Georgetown didn't know what was wrong at first. They came at me with a different version of bad news every hour. First, "We have no idea what has caused this." Not the most reassuring news. So they sent me for a MRI. Then after the MRI, "You have a mass at your waist, and we don't know what it is." So they sent me for a CAT scan because they thought it might be a brain tumor that had dropped down to the spinal cord. By now I was starting to panic. But the CAT scan showed no brain tumor. Then they told me they were going to operate and see what was going on. OK, now I was totally panicked. This sounded much more serious. Up to this point some part of me was still thinking this was something temporary they would fix and I could go home in a day or two…right! I was clueless.

They first inserted five different IVs in my arm and later swapped them out for a humongous needle inserted in the inside of my elbow. I don't remember them inserting any of the needles, and who knew what they were putting in my body—steroids, pain-killer, and what else? I had heard stories about the MRI machine causing people to become claustrophobic, so I made a deal with myself before I went in the tube that I would just meditate and not open my eyes. But once in the tube I was surprised to find it was very noisy, with a lot of banging and bumping sounds. I don't remember being in pain during all these procedures, so I assume I was already doped up.

After the MRI, they took me to Neuro ICU, where I joined three stroke patients. I don't know how anybody survives being a stroke patient! The nurse woke them up every hour to make sure they weren't comatose by shouting their names: "Evelyn, Evelyn, wake up! Squeeze my fingers." Luckily, I had saved the earplugs from the MRI. The night before all this happened I had gone to see the Elizabeth Streb Dance Company at the Kennedy Center. The dancers in the company flew through the air in amazing ways, bouncing off trampolines and enormous cushions. As I lay there in the ICU these images in my head comforted me by distracting me from the horrible situation. I called on those images often in the weeks to come.

By the morning the doctors decided to operate and in preparation for surgery I was to have an angiogram. By now this was getting to be too much for me, and I lost it at the door of the angiogram room and started to sob. I had had three different terrifying diagnoses in eight hours and little sleep. None of my friends were allowed to see me; I was totally isolated and scared to death. I found out later that some of my friends were out in the waiting room, but I didn't know that at the time.

My little meltdown would have been worse if it weren't for my nurse Joseph—an angel in green scrubs. He held me in his arms while I sobbed. When I finally took a breath, he explained there was a small window of opportunity to stop the bleeding before I was totally paralyzed, and that was why they were rushing me around. He continued to check on me the whole time I was in the hospital, even when he wasn't assigned to me. Thank you, Joseph. You saved my sanity.

The angiogram room looked like something out of *Star Trek*. A huge iron lung–like X-ray machine hung from the ceiling with a gurney positioned underneath it. Several people were glued to computer terminals scattered around the room; nobody looked at me. I was exhausted and overwhelmed. It all felt like a bad dream that was happening to someone else. As I laid there on the gurney

I started not caring much what was happening to me. It was too overwhelming, and I was spacing out big time. How else was a girl to cope with a situation like this? It wasn't like they handed me an instruction manual at the door to the ER.

A disembodied voice from the loudspeaker would say, "New road map," and the huge machine swung into action amidst whirling and grunting noises as it changed positions. The loudspeaker would occasionally tell me to hold my breath and not move, and then I would feel a warm gush somewhere on my spine—they were injecting die into the arteries up and down my spinal cord. They finally released me and moved me to a little room nearby. I lay there dreading surgery but when finally one of the doctors came in and told me the diagnosis. It turned out to be an Arterial Venal Malformation (AVM), something very rare for someone my age and rarer too to be located at my waist. It is a condition found usually in young women in their brain and usually fatal. My official designation is incomplete paraplegic (T12). The T12 gives the level of injury, thoracic vertebrae number 12 at my waist, and incomplete means that I am not totally paralyzed. He further explained that they had injected what they called glue powder in the bleeding artery, and no surgery was needed. This procedure was experimental at the time, and he told me that if it held for the next few days, it would hold forever. I was relieved to know that I didn't have to have surgery. That was good news; the rest was still a little dicey.

Later the head neurosurgeon came to talk to me. "If you'd been in a small Midwestern hospital you'd never walk again," he bragged arrogantly. "But you're going to walk with a cane in eight or nine months."

Many years have come and gone since his assurance, and I'm still not walking with a cane. In fact, quite the opposite: I am in the wheelchair full-time. It was really unfair of him to make such a prediction when no one else would. When I'd ask the physical therapists, they'd say, "Well, we'll see. Just keep doing the best you can." I later realized that he could have been correct if I had been allowed to stay at the rehab hospital until I was actually rehabilitated and had access to the physical therapy I needed once I left. But neither of those things happened.

Arrogant neurosurgeons notwithstanding, I am grateful for the boys and their toys; the glue powder treatment saved my ability to walk with a walker for a few years. But their bedside manner sure could have used some improvement. Not one doctor, nurse, medical student, or aide asked me how I felt about what was happening to me. My life had turned upside down, and all they focused on was my physical needs. And no one bothered to tell me what was going to happen to me in the next little while, like going to the Rehab Hospital.

I was at Georgetown Hospital for a week. I was finally allowed visitors and was very glad to see them; one of them organized a twenty-four-hour vigil in the waiting room the first day before they were let into my room. Every time I opened my eyes another gaggle of med students, interns, or residents were coming at me with pins to stick in my legs. I was a rare case who had the misfortune to land in a teaching hospital! Everybody wanted to poke me with a pin to see where I had feeling in my legs, torso, and hips. After the second time I could have told them there was no feeling anywhere below the waist and to stop poking me with that damn pin! It was humiliating to be treated like a specimen. To them, I was just a pair of paralyzed legs, not a fifty-two-year-old biracial lesbian Buddhist community organizer who had led an interesting life.

I quickly learned to become vigilant about my care. I asked to be transferred to a wheelchair, but the person who arrived to do it wasn't well-trained and let me slip right onto the floor. It was a good lesson early in my disability not to put blind faith in anyone. I needed to learn for myself how things should be done. Still, to this day I give very clear instructions when anyone assists me.

Physical therapy began the first day. I was wheeled down to the gym and lined up like for muster in the military. We were the wheelchair lineup of the drugged and disoriented. I seemed to be the only one awake and aware. I suspect the others could have been the same stroke patients the ICU nurses were yelling at! It was a little scary, like a scene from a horror movie where they take people's brains out. My fellow patients weren't even capable of saying, "Good morning," nor could they make eye contact. It was really weird.

My physical therapy aide was an older Russian. A large man, he picked me up out of the wheelchair like I weighed five pounds. It was so reassuring. I felt safe for the first time in days in the arms of a big man like my father. A while later he checked my record, came back, and said, "You're fifty-two? I don't believe it." He made my day.

The PTs loved me. I was awake, alive, and stuffed full of Percocet! In fact, they invited me back after I was out of the hospital to come and talk to them about massage. When I did, I reminded them that they were the only people to touch us without a sharp object in their hand. Touch is so important to healing, but the hospital staff rarely touched you except to do something to you. The Russian holding me in his arms may single-handedly have been responsible for my recovery.

The PTs were pleased that I had strong upper body muscles. I had been working as a massage therapist for a year before this incident, and I could easily transfer myself into a wheelchair within a week. I pressed forty pounds on the lateral press from the beginning. Not to brag or anything, but they thought that was remarkable in a patient my age.

By the end of the week the "glue" was holding, and they transferred me to Mount Vernon Hospital in Virginia, approximately thirty miles from Washington, DC. This was bad news because all my friends lived in DC and Maryland, and moving that far from my support system only increased my isolation. My health insurance company, Kaiser, had a contract with Mount Vernon, so I couldn't go to National Rehabilitation Hospital in DC where I preferred to be. Welcome to the realities of HMOs.

Once again I was loaded into an ambulance, and off we went. The ambulance drivers were clearly related to the good old boys who didn't know how to find Georgetown a week earlier. We left Georgetown and crossed the Key Bridge into Virginia but then looped back across the Roosevelt Bridge into DC and immediately went back to Virginia across the Fourteenth Street Bridge. I said, "You guys only got one more bridge. Are we going to go down to the Wilson Bridge and make it four for four?" After much discussion and argument between the two of them, we eventually found Mount Vernon Hospital. I arrived at Mount Vernon filled with fear and trepidation, as I had very little information about what lay ahead.

Chapter 2

Rehabilitation

I arrived at Mount Vernon Hospital and was put to bed. Someone had thoughtfully left a wheelchair beside it. I transferred into my wheelchair and went out to see what was happening. I surprised a nurse at the nursing station.

"What are you doing out here?" she said.

"I came to see what's going on"," I said.

"You're not allowed to transfer into your wheelchair!"

"Well, nobody told me. I know how to do it."

"No, you don't; go back to bed! You are not allowed to transfer yourself until the doctor authorizes it."

How silly was that? Well, this was just the beginning of a life where the world was no longer my oyster. From now on someone else would decide when I would get up, what time I would eat, and what I would do all day. And once I got out of the rehab hospital a number of agencies were going to set limits on me. From now on everyone will be keen to tell me what I could do and not do.

Someone, for instance, would hamper my entrance to a building by not providing a ramp. Someone else would limit my access to transportation by imposing restrictive criteria for paratransit services. Someone else would put a ceiling on my earnings and penalize me if I disobeyed the rules. Someone else would curb my choices of where to live by refusing to build accessible apartments. Many of the freedoms I enjoyed as an able-bodied individual were about to disappear from my life in a curious intersection of disability and poverty. But I digress.

Back at the hospital, I had no idea what lay ahead. I had six short weeks to learn everything I needed to know about being disabled. I found out later that before HMOs dominated the health care system, someone with an injury like mine would stay four months in a rehab facility. Needless to say, I was not rehabilitated in six weeks—not even close.

But given who I was, I plunged in, eager to find out how to do everything from a wheelchair. I wanted to know how to transfer in and out of my chair, the shower, or a car. I wanted to learn how to pop a wheelie over a curb, how to open a door and get the wheelchair through the doorframe, and how to get back into my wheelchair should I fall out. It was clear that there was a lot to learn: how to manage my partially paralyzed bladder and bowels, how to use a kitchen while sitting down, and even how to carry things in a wheelchair. My self-esteem had taken a huge blow, and I overcompensated by becoming competent in my new world. I had no time to be sitting around bemoaning my fate! I had things to learn, curbs to conquer, bladders to control. I was very busy in the rehab hospital.

But the hospital had its problems. I was the victim of a conflict of agendas. The ward staff had an interest in keeping us in bed, out of the way, and with few individual demands. They wanted us there at their convenience, lying in bed when they arrived with food, the meds, or a pan of cold water to wash up with. It would be a lot easier on them if we were not underfoot out in the ward. The facility was designed for the convenience of the medical staff, and only one floor was used for rehabilitation. On the other hand, the therapists pushed us to be independent by teaching us to use our wheelchairs. Had these folks designed the facility, life would have been very different.

The fact that I was a high-functioning paraplegic was a problem for the ward staff. The majority of the patients were not able to get out of bed on their own. Unlike the rest of them, I had had no injury or surgery from which to recover. I was in better shape physically upon arrival than most patients—not to mention I was of a very independent nature to start with. I found myself running afoul of the rules more often than not. I was a self-sufficient round peg smashing up against a very square hole. This has continued to be a struggle. I am still the intelligent, capable woman I was before this all happened to me, yet I am continually treated as though I am brainless and not capable of blowing my own nose. When I met my new internist recently I told her we would get along great as long as she never treated me like a little old lady in a wheelchair! I see myself as an Amazon who just happens to use a wheelchair to get around.

One of the more serious struggles with spinal cord injuries is waste management. Bladder and bowel control are key to survival. If you are paralyzed and your waste systems are off-line, manual systems have to replace the natural ones. As the first line of offense, they insert a tube (catheter) into your bladder and drain the urine out into a bag. Some paralyzed people remain at this stage the rest of their lives. Others are fortunate enough to be able to use the catheter intermittently and insert it only when they need to empty their bladder. I was lucky enough to finally be able to void on my own by pressing my hand down on my bladder and leaning forward, but I have to wear pads because I am not always aware of when I need to urinate.

The first day they installed a Foley catheter, which stayed in all the time, because I was then totally incontinent. One day the nurse was having trouble inserting the catheter. Another nurse came by to help and then a third. There they were, the three of them poking around my private parts. I smiled to my old dyke self and thought, *Well, in other circumstances I might enjoy this!* I also thought, *How hard can it be to find where to put it?*

After two weeks in the hospital, they started to teach me to "cath" myself, and I found out how hard it could be…. What a pain in the ass! I had to use sterile gloves, which are packaged in paper and had to be opened in a certain sequence so as not to contaminate them. Once I got the gloves on, I couldn't touch anything, so I had to remember to open everything I needed before I put them on. It was very anxiety producing. Once the gloves were on I had to clean the area with icky iodine stuff. To be able to see where to insert the tube into my urethra, a very, very small opening, about the size of a lentil, I had to balance a mirror on a brace between my knees. Are you getting the picture here? I had to coordinate about 30 things at the same time, adjust the mirror, get it to hold still between my knees (I did mention that my legs are paralyzed, right?), insert the tube into a tiny little hole that you can barely see (and I have no feeling there, so I have no idea where I am putting the damn thing), and if I was lucky enough to find the correct hole (the vagina and the anus are in same region), I had to remember to put the other end of the catheter in the bottle or the pee spilled out all over the bed. Yikes! All this and remembering not to contaminate the gloves. I did finally learn to cath, but luckily after a few weeks my body cooperated and started voiding itself. Thank god.

They were also keen to establish a bowel program for me. The theory is that your body would like to have a bowel movement at the same time every day. So they would give me a suppository every day at the same time in the hopes that my body would get the message. One day the suppository wasn't working, so they gave me another…and then forgot about me. An hour or so later, a chaplain, who I did not know, poked her head around the curtain to say hello. Well, my body decided to greet her with a three-day supply of poop that shot out all over the bed, stinking to high heaven. I was so embarrassed, and so was she, but what are you going to do? Suck it up and cry into your pillow at night.

My bowels finally settled into a routine, and now I "digitally disimpact," which means put on gloves, apply a little lubricant, stick my finger up my butt, and fish out the feces. I have no real sensation about when to go, so I do it every day at the same time. Doing it right after you eat is very helpful; dogs know this, which is why they want to go out right after you feed them.

My first day at Mount Vernon was celebrated by starting my period. It was totally unexpected, as I was in the throes of menopause. But I looked down, and there was blood all over my legs. A male nurse answered the call button…. Eww! There went every last expectation of modesty and privacy. Not to mention that I was a lesbian! It was just so wrong to me to have a man clean up my menstrual blood. Sacred blood is a woman thing. No men allowed. Yet there I was lying in bed, and a man was washing me up.

I was to have a shower every other day, and coming from Hawaii, where we sometimes shower twice a day, I really looked forward to it. But in reality I got a shower about every three days, and then the aide would try to hurry me up. Most of my washing up took place in my bed.

Because I was doing so well in my recovery, they put me in a room off of the day room that was separated from the main ward. In the past they had used this room to get people ready to go home. I was very lonely and isolated there. I only had two roommates who were each there for a brief stay. One was a young woman who had experienced a stroke; she was there only a week. My other roommate was also a young woman, who suffered from juvenile diabetes. At age thirty she was already blind and a double amputee. Her husband had died recently of AIDS, and she was in the hospital to learn independent living skills. The aides who cleaned the room evidently did not have any training on assisting blind individuals or didn't care. They moved her belongings every day when they cleaned and did not put them back where she could find them. She would return from physical therapy and not be able to find essential things like the sliding board that she needed to transfer into bed. Each day I would help her rearrange the room back to the way she wanted it. The kitchen help wasn't any better; they would drop off her dinner tray and leave. She was blind! Someone, kitchen staff, aide, or nurse, should have made sure she knew where everything was on the tray. I would go over and point out where everything was. Her future seemed even more precarious, as she was to move in with her two really weird bachelor brothers. They were to have remodeled their house for her but hadn't by the time she was discharged. She wouldn't survive long in that environment.

I liked my doctor, Stephanie Giolando, D.O., very much. She stopped by every day. I really enjoyed my talks with her, and she never seemed in a hurry. Her visit was the highlight of my day. Since she was a Doctor of Osteopathy I offered my body for a spinal adjustment, but she said that she didn't do that anymore. Too bad. We had a number of issues to resolve in a short period of time. Pain management was the first item of business. She had wanted to put me on time-release Percocet but it wasn't available in that hospital, so she settled for time-release morphine. I am not sure what the difference between the two drugs is, but I was on the morphine for nine months.

The pain was intense at first. They put me on a six-hour dose of Percocet. It would wear off in four hours, and I had to sit there in pain for two horrible hours before they would give me more. In those two hours I was immobilized by the pain. I would sit there frozen and pant. My brain would numb. Finally they switched me to time-release morphine. It's wonderful stuff. I'd missed the drug scene in my youth, and like Bill Clinton I had never inhaled! I just wasn't interested in drugs and alcohol as a young person. But one day in the hospital I looked out the window and got totally lost in the clouds. And morphine, strangely enough, removed an inhibition about drawing. Before the morphine I could barely draw a stick figure; now I could draw an accurate representation of my wheelchair, along with several other things in my room.

Several bodyworker friends came to the hospital to treat me. In my work as a massage therapist I had become acquainted with a number of practitioners. Nancy Shaw, a trigger point therapist, tried to relieve the spasms in my legs. Jane Pennington, a longtime friend and amateur masseuse, massaged my legs. Meade Andrews, an Alexander Technique teacher, also worked with me.

Completely opposite from my bodyworker friends, no one touched me in the hospital without hurting me. No one rubbed my back. My mother was a nurse in the fifties and sixties, and she spoke often of giving someone a massage. The nurse's aides looked as though they'd sooner kill me. The nurses were way too busy for hand-holding. They would rush in my room, ask me something, give me a pill, and rush out. The PTs did touch me a lot, but it was to steady me, keep me from falling, stretching a muscle, and so on, which helped some, but it wasn't like being touched affectionately. But my friends knew what was needed and provided me with lots of touch and affection when they came to visit. It really made a difference to me and counteracted the cold, hard reality of the hospital. Meade once brought a copy of the movie *Fly Away Home*. She hauled the big TV from the day room into my room and piled into bed with me to watch it. It was the best thing. We interpreted the film for my blind roommate, describing what we saw. She really enjoyed it too.

I badly needed to process what was going on emotionally as well. I had been a Re-evaluation Counselor since 1994 and was still active in the local Re-evaluation Counseling (RC) community. Re-evaluation Counseling is a worldwide movement of peer counselors. It is based on the idea that we are all born good and learn behaviors to survive childhood and then cling to what we learned then even though it may not work so well once we are grown. The evaluation part is going back to see just what we learned and updating it so it works for us as adults. My co-counselor came to the hospital and sat directly in front of me, held both my hands in hers, and leaned in close to my face. Looking me right in the eye, she encouraged me to re-tell the story of my trauma. As I told the story I cried and cried. She would stop me if I rushed past a painful part, encouraging me to pause and feel what was going on. I think RC is the most effective counseling technique ever invented. Check it out http://www.rc.org. I had used the same technique two years earlier when I was diagnosed with breast cancer. The RC community had rallied to my side and provided me with a month of daily counseling. I breezed through the breast cancer treatment with flying colors.

The counseling support provided by the psychologist on the ward was a joke. He came to my room on the second day and asked what he could do to make my stay more comfortable. I said I was a lesbian and would appreciate being connected with other gay patients or staff. He was nonplussed! I could tell my request shocked him, and needless to say he never did anything about it. He was also leader of the so-called coping skills group, which met every Thursday afternoon. He was the worst group facilitator I had ever encountered. We sat in a circle, and he had us share our names and diagnosis but nothing further. There we were about ten of us with a wide variety of disabilities, including a woman who had had a heart transplant, a guy with huge swollen legs, my blind roommate, an older man with a broken neck, and a young man who had had a stroke. The psychologist started up right after the introductions by asking: "What is your biggest fear?" You should have seen the look of disbelief ricocheting around the group. There was an instant nonverbal agreement in the room for dead silence. We did not know each other, and we were not going to share our worst fears with one another or with him. He waited for a short ten seconds and said, "When I've done these groups before, people tell me their biggest fear is falling out of their wheelchairs." The group jumped on this enthusiastically: "Oh, yes, that's right." Our lives were turned upside down, our careers down the toilet, our families altered forever, our self-images smashed to bits, and he thought our worst fear was falling out of a wheelchair? Not even!

What did work, however, were the physical, occupational, and recreational therapies. I had a very active daily schedule and loved having something to do. But more importantly, I had a sense of making progress in learning things about my altered life. I liked that there were tangible things I could do to counteract what had been done to me. A sense of self-reliance and determination set in. I may have lost the use of my legs, but by god, I could learn to get in and out of the shower. In a strange way, each little thing I learned to do worked to ameliorate the devastation. I couldn't walk, but I could press forty pounds on the weight lifting machine. It wasn't logical or rational; a shift in identity was taking place in a deep crevasse in my soul. I had been a tall, strong, athletic woman for fifty-two years, and now I needed to reconcile the reality of my limp legs with that image. I grew up in Hawaii on the ocean. I was a surfer, a skin diver, and I crewed on racing sailboats. I took a five-day backpacking trip from the summit of Haleakala to Seven

Sacred Pools when I was thirty. And now I could not fricking stand up!

The expectation that I would, of course, cope magnificently was huge. It was both my own expectation and that of others around me. Letting this defeat me was unthinkable. I pushed myself to do well in everything they put in front of me. A man in his early thirties joined me in physical therapy the third week. He had meningitis and was just recovering his strength. He couldn't stand it that an old lady (in his eyes) was doing more than he could. I was three weeks ahead of him, and he worked really hard to catch up to me. It worked both ways; I worked really hard to keep ahead of him. A win-win situation.

Five days a week, first thing in the morning I had mat group. We got to move on the mat in ways that were impossible in a hospital bed, and the aides manually stretched our paralyzed parts. It was one of my favorite activities. It was fun, it felt good to stretch, and I got to have social contact with the other patients, a rare event. After mat group came one hour of physical therapy, where we worked on strengthening my legs and relearning basic coordination. Several days a week were dedicated to wheelchair training, where I learned how to transfer into my wheelchair safely, get back into my wheelchair should I fall out, and how to get over curbs. I had weight training every other day to build up the strength in my arms. Occupational therapy (OT) involved teaching me how to transfer into and out of a car and the shower and how to cook from a wheelchair. Recreation therapy took us out of the hospital to learn how to make our way in a store or movie theater. I was busy five hours a day. It felt good to be engaged, to learn things I knew I would need to know. It was tiring, but it felt good. Plus it distracted me from lying around wondering what would happen to me.

One day at mat group an older man with a wood and metal "halo" frame used to hold his head and neck in place was being transferred to the mat by an aide. Just as she got her head under his arm, he went into a spasm, and his arm clamped down on her head. She was yelling for him to let go, he was yelling that he couldn't, and they tumbled down on the mat like wrestlers. The rest of us were laughing so hard we could barely breathe. Mat group was fun and very informal, as opposed to almost everything else we did.

My PT was a recent graduate and very enthusiastic. She taught me how to get down the stairs backward in my wheelchair by holding on to the rail and slowly lowering myself down. She taught me how to get up the stairs by getting out of my wheelchair and pulling it up after me. She taught me how to "pop a wheelie," a technique used to get over curbs...not as easy as it seems. You have to have enough forward momentum to get the big wheel to bounce over the curb and the coordination just right to pop your front caster wheels high enough in the air to clear the curb. So you have to roll forward and at the same time lean back so your front wheels come off the ground without tipping over backward. So there we were out in the parking lot practicing popping wheelies at the curb. I banged into the curb repeatedly, not able to get the timing quite right. A kindly older gentleman came over to me and pointed out that there was a curb cut just twenty feet away and why didn't I use it? I told him my PT wouldn't let me go to lunch until I figured out how to get over the curb!

The first day in the wheelchair class they dumped me over (gently) and told me to get back up. No instructions, just get back up.... It was hard, but I did have strong arms and managed to do it. They gave me the instructions after I had figured it out for myself. They didn't treat everyone like this; I think they knew I learned better doing it myself. They also put a ten-pound weight on the bottom of my wheelchair and sent me around the carpeted lobby to build up my arms. Some could call that abuse!

In OT I had to learn to get in and out of a car. They had a complete car in the gym; it just didn't have a motor. The OT, a stern dominatrix (in a good way), took me over to the car, opened the driver's door, and said get in and bring your wheelchair in behind you. She must have been talking to the wheelchair class folks, because that was all the instruction she gave me! Not one to turn down a challenge, I got in. It didn't take long to figure out how to dismantle the wheelchair and pull it in piece by piece. After tackling that successfully, she sent me out to see how I could deal with the public bathroom in the lobby, which was mostly inaccessible. She said I would encounter this situation over and over out in the world, and she was right. I found OT very helpful, as it was all practical stuff.

Recreational therapy was also very helpful, and I could have used more of it. Two RTs took me for a swim at a local public pool that had a ramp right down into the water. We used a plastic wheelchair and rolled in to where I could float out of the chair. They worked with me while I exercised in the water and then told me I could paddle around if I wanted. Well…I am an excellent swimmer, so I took off down the lane doing the crawl with just my arms. Neither of them swam well, and they shouted at me to come back until they realized that I was not endangering myself. It felt really good to be in the water—wonderful stress relief for me. And God knows this whole experience was stressful. I spent my childhood in, on, or next to the ocean. My family had a fishing skiff and a small sailboat, and my Godfather had a forty-foot ketch that I crewed on throughout my teenage years. I think I may have been a dolphin in a past life; the water is a huge comfort to me. I continue to swim several days a week even now.

They also took several of us out in van to the movies so we could figure out how to manage popcorn and a drink without spilling it all over ourselves. It was a good introduction on how to get in and out of a van, how to manage curb cuts in a parking lot, and how to open heavy doors. It was also a good introduction into the attitudes of the nondisabled community. People were impatient for us to get through the lines and out of their way. The theater seats set aside for us were in the front row right next to the screen. I had not sat in those seats since I was seven…and the thrill of sitting so close had long disappeared.

All of the physical training was good, but the best information I received was from a nurse practitioner assigned to instruct me in Spinal Cord Injury 101. She normally taught a class, but I was the only spinal cord injured (SCI) patient at the time, so I had individual sessions. She led me through a series of workshops on managing the bladder and bowels, the hazards of pressure sores, what danger signs of other medical conditions to look for, preventing shoulder injury while using a wheelchair, coping skills to avoid depression, and how to manage in a household. It was a very helpful series, and she was an excellent teacher. I left with some confidence that I could manage, and I knew that I could call her if I had a question.

Near the end of my time there, I finally managed to stand on one leg by myself. It was a cause for great celebrating. My PT was elated and gave me a big hug, and all the other patients were cheering. It was like being a baby, learning to walk all over again— a big fuss over baby's first step! Standing is a very helpful function to recover. It is not healthy to sit all the time; your organs get squished and don't work right. Muscles and tendons tighten up, and circulation is hampered, so being able to stand is a very good thing. It also reduces an inaccessible world to one you can manage. You can, for instance, get out of your chair to get up steps, and you can stand to reach things on upper shelves. It made my life in the wheelchair a little easier.

I was absent from my room a lot, and my friends had a hard time reaching me on the phone. One friend had the good idea to bring an answering machine so people could leave messages. I had been receiving a lot of calls, and it was exhausting to repeat the same thing over and over to each caller. But with the answering machine I could leave an updated message every day, like "Today for the first time I pulled myself to an upright position on the parallel bars," or "Today I learned how to put on my socks." I asked them to leave a message and told them I would not call them back unless they needed me to. I received several affirming messages a day. It was great.

Since the hospital was thirty miles from DC, not many people came to visit me during the week. My friend Stanley showed up like clockwork on Thursdays and usually finished my dinner. Other friends brought me clothes and fish sandwiches from McDonald's. I had a lot of visitors on Saturdays and Sundays who were all eager to get me up and out. As soon as I had permission to leave the floor, I did.

One visitor I always looked forward to was Esme Farb. Esme was born deaf and with cerebral palsy, and at age twenty she was involved in a traffic accident that left her brain-injured and quadriplegic. I told Esme that she must now become my mentor and teach me how to be good "crip." I knew from her mother,

Judith Treesberg, that being disabled was a political statement as well as a medical condition. I had worked for civil rights of others all my life, and now I was joining yet another group whose civil rights were regularly violated. I also knew that there was special etiquette that I needed learn about how to communicate with deaf individuals, how to assist a blind person if he or she needs help, and everything else about the politics of being disabled. Esme had her aide bring her over a couple times, and we talked about life in the wheelchair. She was really helpful to me, and I am grateful for her assistance. She and Judith provided a good introduction to my new world of disabilities that was not available from the hospital staff. I found out later that the Centers for Independent Living can provide the same information that Judith and Esme provided me. You can locate one near you at http://www.ncil.org.

I've always been an outgoing and gregarious person and thought of myself as someone who would be there for my friends if they needed me. I did not really give any thought to whether the reverse was true. Before my disability I had thought of myself as someone who takes care of others, but there I was, in need of help and getting it. I had been totally unaware that I had a circle of friends who would respond positively to my altered state. In some ways accepting the love and attention of my friends was harder than being crippled. I had more than one good cry about it. It was just the beginning of redefining parts of my identity.

My six-week stay was too short, and I would have been in much better shape for all that faced me if I had been allowed to stay longer. It is, in my opinion, the greed of HMOs like Kaiser that shortened my stay at the hospital It was not a medical consideration, I was told by a nurse that in years past someone with my level of injury would stay four months. The policy made my life really hard for the first few months I was out on my own, and in fact Kaiser probably would have saved thousands of dollars over the years if I had known more about my disability before I was discharged. Better training would have prevented a number of expensive mishaps. I suppose this will fall on deaf ears, as nothing speaks louder than money.

When it came time to be discharged, the hospital social worker was of little help. She was swamped. I asked her to explain Social Security benefits to me, and she gave me an 800 number to call. I was discharged with no information about how to get a handicap tag for my car, how to sign up for Metro access paratransit service, how to get a half-price bus card, how to find accessible housing, or how to apply for SSDI. If it hadn't been for my friends Judith and Esme I would never have known any of those things.

I will end the story of my time in the rehab hospital with a complaint. The nurse aides on my ward were all from the Caribbean and mean as hell to me. I have been to Jamaica and have had Jamaican friends. My friends were sweet, friendly people. But these aides were not. They were overworked and underpaid. They had too many patients assigned to them. The nurses were also overworked, and the atmosphere was toxic. The aides would talk to one another right over the top of me, never acknowledging that I existed. Before I was "allowed" to transfer, one of them left me on the toilet for twenty minutes. I "illegally" transferred myself off the toilet and went to look for her. I found her at the nurse's station chatting with the other aides. I gave her a piece of my mind. Later she came into my room and threatened me against ever daring to publicly humiliate her again. It was a little scary, as I was at her mercy.

I mention this in the hopes that some hospital administrator will read this and have a new understanding about how their policies affect patients. I think most people think the nurses are the most important resource on the ward, but in fact patients spend almost all their time with the aides. We were devastated from a major life trauma, and the shock of it had turned our lives upside down, but instead of a peaceful, healing atmosphere, we were subjected to hostile, overworked women who treated us as though they hated our guts. The nursing staff was so busy they had no time to spend with us. In my six weeks there I had only one conversation with a nurse that wasn't directly related to something they wanted me to do or something I wanted to have done.

In an ideal world, I would have been assigned to a hospital that was designed for rehab, stayed for four months until I could walk with a walker and take care of myself, and been surrounded by competent psychological help and sweet, friendly nurse aides who actually cared whether I recovered or not. But you make do with what you have, for you will suffer in life to the same degree you wish things were different.

Chapter 3

The Dawn of a New Age

Upon discharge from Mount Vernon Hospital, I was launched out into a new world quite unprepared for what I would have to deal with. On that day I could stand on one leg shaking like a leaf, I barely had control of my bladder and had no wheelchair of my own, and until two days before discharge I had no place to go. I did not know how to get my car adapted with hand controls, had no idea what I needed to remodel in my apartment, no idea how to get ramps installed, no idea how I was going to make a living, and no idea at all how I was going to cope with all this. Good thing I was seriously doped up on painkillers, or I might have panicked.

Esme, my quadriplegic friend and mentor, invited me to share her two-bedroom accessible apartment. She had an aide to cook meals and do light housekeeping. But it didn't work out. It had a deep carpet that was very difficult to roll around on (Esme had a motorized chair), and the bathroom I was to use really wasn't accessible. I stayed only two days. But the real reason, I think, was that I was a wreck emotionally and physically. I needed someone

33

to take care of me, and living in Esme's apartment required me to be more independent than I was ready to be.

Luckily my friends Helen and Donna offered me an accessible room in their large house. There was a bedroom and bath just behind the dining room. It had been servants' quarters when the house was built in the twenties. It was all on one level and had wood floors that were easy to roll around on. Helen had been a rehab nurse years earlier, and both she and Donna were warm, nurturing people who made me feel very welcome. I don't know what I would have done without them.

There is no answer to the question "why did this happen to me?" but it is possible to take the edge off of it. This was a catastrophe in the truest sense of the word: *a calamity, an event resulting in great loss and misfortune, a state of extreme ruin and misfortune.* Everything I had known about myself was no longer true. I began to realize that clinging to what I used to be was a recipe for disaster. I had been studying Buddhism for several years, and I was about to be handed a lesson about the self, as my self as I had known it was now destroyed. Who was I without my body? The phoenix had burst into flames and was about to be reborn.

It was summer, and Helen's garden outside my window was beautiful. Blue and white flowers bordered bright green grass, a white fence, and a tall stand of trees. The sight was very peaceful; I looked at it for hours.

Helen was the perfect nurse. She worked from home as a consultant and was available to give me a hand. On the first or second day I peed in the bed, and I rolled out to the kitchen and asked for something to clean it up. Helen said she would clean it up. "No," I said, "It's my mess, and I will clean it up." She then told me that she was the nurse, so she knew how to clean it up and I didn't. She poured a glass of water on the stain and then absorbed it with two very thick towels. It worked; there was no stain left and no odor. I also developed the beginnings of a pressure sore in a day from the mattress. Helen provided a sheepskin pad for me to sleep on giving me with an important lesson on how to manage one aspect of my disability.

At this point in my rehabilitation, things alternated between being just way too much to deal with and an interesting challenge to see what I could do in my altered state. My disability had taken all spontaneity out of my life. Everything, every little thing, like getting from the bed to the wheelchair, now needed a plan, and at times I was just not up to it. And I was constantly surprised by what I did not know.

One day I made myself a baked potato in the microwave. I took the cooked potato out of the microwave and put it on a plate in my lap. Unbeknownst to me, the hot potato gave me a second-degree burn about the size of a quarter on my thigh. It was another lesson not learned at the hospital; we had to demonstrate we could cook there, but nobody said anything about potato safety!

Prior to my disability I had been active for many years with the Mary-Helen Mautner Project for Lesbians with Cancer, a local cancer service organization. They had no clients at the time, so I became their client of sorts. I was assigned a coordinator to whom I gave my weekly schedule. She arranged rides to my appointments and told me who would pick me up. It was great service; it allowed me to get out, to have company, and to take advantage of a lot of alternative treatments that I wouldn't have been able to get to otherwise. I was going to physical therapy twice a week and acupuncture and massage once a week.

Two volunteers from the Mautner Project came to build ramps so I could get in and out of the house easily. They were amateur carpenters who had never built a ramp before, but they set about the task with great enthusiasm. As they were working I decided to show off my newly gained skill of rolling myself backward down the steps in my wheelchair. I carefully lowered myself down the first six steps amidst much encouragement, but the bottom step was curved outward, and I was flung out expectedly onto the lawn. I lay in the grass laughing, and the carpenters were horrified. Pride goeth before the fall! Once they realized I wasn't hurt they joined in laughing. I am sure it became quite a story all over DC.

The residence of the Egyptian ambassador was located at the end of our street. One day I was rolling myself down to the corner for exercise when one of the men working there came over and tried to tell me something. He didn't speak English, and I didn't speak Arabic. He kept pointing to my house and patting his shoulders. I didn't understand, and his intensity scared me a little. So I just kept saying no and rolled back home. A week or so later, I ran into a woman who also lived there and told her about the incident. She said he was a massage therapist and was offering to massage me. I felt so embarrassed that I didn't understand what the man had been offering, and a massage would have been nice.

Due to an administrative screwup at Kaiser, I sat idle for one month with no physical therapy after I was discharged from the hospital. Helen and I did what exercises we could think of, but finally, at Helen's urging, I wrote a letter to the customer service complaint department. In twenty-four hours I had an appointment. Kaiser granted me eight weeks in private PT. It was the best PT I had ever had, before or after. My PT was an older woman who had worked in Israel during the Six-Day War. She had quite a bag of tricks of how to do PT without any equipment. The things she had me do were very clever, including using my hair dryer to dry out my pressure sore so it healed up immediately.

At the end of the eight weeks, they transferred me to Kaiser PT. Dr. Giolando wrote on my discharge papers that I needed daily PT for the rest of my life, but Kaiser only authorized eight weeks! But with the collusion of my therapist, it was eighteen months before the administrators figured out I was still there. Somebody was on my side! I realize now that if I had been allowed to stay at the hospital for three or four months and had a more aggressive physical therapy program when I got out, I probably could have walked with a cane like the neurosurgeon predicted. But I didn't have the money for private physical therapy, nor did I understand the importance of daily exercise at the time, so I let it slide.

My days at Helen and Donna's were peaceful and healing. They provided just the right amount of nurture and care to allow me to recover. I didn't have to go shopping or do anything to manage my household. I only had to make my own breakfast. Helen, especially, provided me with much-needed company, as I was becoming increasingly more isolated.

After I had been at Helen and Donna's for three months, Donna was diagnosed with breast cancer. I decided to move back home, because I knew then that my presence was an intrusion into their privacy. I was ready to go. I could stand on both legs, make my way up a few steps, and walk a short distance with a walker. I had become better adjusted to the morphine and could function better cognitively than I had earlier.

I had been involved with alternative healing treatments for many years. After the rehab hospital I set about developing a mind, body, and spirit regime to heal my broken body. At the time of my catastrophe I was already receiving treatments from a chiropractor, massage therapist, acupuncturist, and a nutritionist. The chiropractor gently worked my misaligned spine back into place with massage. My massage therapist provided much-needed primal maternal touch that comforted me like one would comfort a newborn baby. I was being reborn; everything about my life had changed and was now new.

My recovery was greatly enhanced by the acupuncture I received at the very capable hands of Alaine Duncan at Crossings, A Center for the Healing Traditions in Silver Spring, Maryland. I had started treatment with her in 1995 for my breast cancer and had gone to her regularly ever since. It is very hard to describe the exact benefits, but I know it was central to my healing. I always felt more balanced after a treatment, and I think the balance allowed all my systems to function efficiently and let my body heal itself. Whether it was the treatment or Alaine's amazing, warm attention to me, I can't say, but it worked.

I had been under the care of nutritionist Richard Power for several years, and his amazing knowledge of supplements and vitamins was also very helpful to me. The least helpful in all this was my physiatrist (a physical medicine doctor) at Kaiser. He answered cell phone calls from his mother in the middle of my appointments, and he talked incessantly about coaching his daughter's soccer team. He was a tall, lanky, low-energy fellow who never seemed busy like other doctors. He did nothing for me himself; he just referred me to other doctors and in no way was any help to either my physical or spiritual healing. I think he may have been related to the psychologist at the rehab hospital, brothers or something....

I moved back to my apartment, and the same friends who built the ramps at Helen and Donna's built a ramp into my apartment building. My building had a good-sized step at the entrance and four steps from the foyer to my apartment on the first floor. I could now walk up the steps and use a walker around my apartment.

Every bit of equipment I've needed appeared in a timely fashion and usually for free. A friend with post-polio syndrome gave me her old wheelchair. It was too small, but I didn't realize at the time that wheelchairs were fitted to your height and weight. Someone who'd been in a traffic accident gave me a walker she no longer needed; she called it "Alice Walker." Alice went with me everywhere—into the ocean, across the lava on a trip to Hawaii, and into the shower in an inaccessible bathroom. Another friend gave me an electric scooter that her mother had used before she died. It was an indoor scooter with small tires, and it wasn't long before I tore it up on the sidewalks and had to trade it in. I purchased it myself, unaware that Voc Rehab would purchase it for me. I asked them for a wheelchair and hand controls, but I don't know why I didn't ask for a scooter.

But I didn't ask. Instead, a fierce independence set in. Every little thing was a challenge, and I was up to the challenge! I had something to prove. That little blood vessel may have taken my legs, but by God, I was still powerful and independent and set out to prove it.

In the fall of 1997, my good friend Bente Cooney offered me a part-time job at the National Osteoporosis Foundation (NOF). At the time the Social Security Administration allowed me a trial work period to see if I could go back to work full time. I was allowed to earn all I could for nine months and was not subject to the $500-a-month limit imposed on people who depend exclusively on Social Security Disability Insurance. It quickly became apparent that I could not work full time. I was still on time-release morphine, which took care of the pain in my abdomen, but I still had neuropathic pain in my legs. The pain limited my energy, and the morphine troubled my concentration. I worked at NOF for several months but finally gave up the job to my friend Esther Katzman, who did a great job after I left.

For the first year or two it was very exciting to figure out how to do almost everything, but it wore thin after a while. I didn't exactly get depressed, but I certainly slowed down. The drugs used to control the neuropathic pain in my legs were troublesome for me. In the four years between 1998 and 2002, I was prescribed Neurontin, Elavil, and Lyrica. These are helpful drugs for some, but for me they were horrible. They controlled the pain, but "I" left the planet. If I was not engaged in a conversation or task, I was drowsing in my chair. I would get up after sleeping twelve hours, eat breakfast and take a nap, wake up, eat lunch, take a nap, eat dinner, and sleep in the chair in front of the TV until bedtime. Hardly a life.

The doctors and I tried one drug after the other, different doses, and finally going without drugs, which wasn't much of a solution, as I was in quite a bit of pain. We finally settled on oral Baclofen, a muscle relaxant, which worked OK, but I was still drowsier than I wanted to be. In 2001 my neurologist, tired, I suspect, of hearing me complain, suggested an intrathecal device. It is a pump about the size of a tuna fish can inserted under the skin of the abdomen that delivers a small, steady dose of medicine into my spinal fluid (Read more about the pump in Chapter 6, Pain and Suffering).

In 1998 I approached Voc Rehab about going back to school. I had a Master's in Social Work, but I had focused on the community organizing aspects of the field, and now I wanted to become a therapist. I enrolled in George Washington University and received an Education Specialist (EdS) degree in Rehabilitation Counseling in 2000. I was offered the opportunity to study for a PhD. I took all the coursework and internships for a PhD, but I didn't have to do a dissertation. I am a clinician, not a researcher, it was a good compromise. Voc Rehab not only paid my tuition but also gave me a stipend for books and transportation while I attended classes. Not a bad deal! And for once the world of disabilities worked the way it was supposed to. They provided me the means to change to a career I could do from a wheelchair, and I have been earning my living with it ever since.

I loved being in school. I was older than almost all the students and some of the faculty. I especially enjoyed my classes with Maureen

McGuire-Kuletz and appreciated her friendship for years after. She had come to teaching from the trenches, where she managed a Voc Rehab system in Virginia. She had a very different understanding of the real world. There were no disabled faculty teaching in the Rehabilitation Counseling courses and only one other disabled student, a man who was blind. I provided as much information about what life was like in a wheelchair for my fellow students, but it should have come from the faculty. But they weren't disabled...see the problem?

My counseling classes were a breeze. After years of training in Re-evaluation Counseling, I felt like I was just going through the motions of learning to counsel. I was already a very competent counselor when I arrived, but I needed a credential. I was open to learning a new way to counsel. My technique now is eclectic: a little RC, a smattering of Jungian psychology, and the counseling techniques they taught at GWU.

I learned about Jungian psychology with Janice Taylor, a therapist whom I saw on a regular basis from 2000 to 2002. Her work with me on separating a behavior I had learned as a child from thinking it was an attribute of my personality was a groundbreaking discovery for me. It literally changed my life. And it was a tremendously important discovery, as I was essentially reinventing my identity as a person with a disability in every other way.

This was also a rich spiritual time for me. I describe the details of these experiences throughout this book. I went on a silent retreat in the fall of 1997, which I describe in the chapter "Not So Silent Retreat." In "Moments of Grace" I tell you about a retreat with Bobby Rhodes, a Zen teacher from Providence, Rhode Island, where I encountered the divine universe. Everything I thought was me, it turned out, was irrelevant. Stripped down to the barest bone, all pretenses set aside, I evidently was not that tall, athletic woman who had worked for the national offices of women's organizations. I was instead a short woman in a wheelchair, scraping by with part-time work taking a magnificent spiritual journey.

By 2001 I was working part time for the Disability Rights Council (DRC), assisting Linda Royster and the attorneys in preparing lawsuits against businesses that violated the Americans with Disabilities Act. I researched the violations by getting in my scooter and visiting the store, restaurant, or hotel to assess the situation. The DRC was a project of the Washington Lawyers Committee for Civil Rights and Urban Affairs, a coalition of lawyers who cared about justice. The member firms provided pro bono attorneys to try the cases. They were usually young and enthusiastic and a lot of fun to work with. We took on CVS drugstores, Popeye's, and a series of locally owned hotels. We settled every case in our favor. While I was staying overnight in one of the hotels, a faulty shower bench collapsed, and I broke my tailbone. The young attorneys were stoked! Not only did we nail the hotel for the ADA violations, but they got me $12,000 in damages, all for a broken tailbone I did not feel.

I also worked one day a week as a counselor to the staff of the ENDependence Center of Northern Virginia in Arlington. ECNV is a center for independent living, an agency set up to serve people with disabilities. This was my immersion into the world of disabilities. Almost everyone on the staff was a person with a disability. I really enjoyed working with them and they taught me a lot. If you are a person newly disabled, contact your local Center for Independent Living. They can guide you through the morass of agencies you will need to deal with. To find your local CIL, Contact the National Council on Independent Living, http://www.ncil.org/

In 2000 I went on a retreat to Mexico sponsored by my friend Meade Andrews. There I met a woman who I thought at the time was the one I had waited for my entire life. And for two years I thought this was good. She lived about an hour's drive from DC, so I saw her only on the weekends. It was a schedule that worked for me. I spent a few minutes each day on the phone maintaining my relationship and had someone to play with on the weekends. It turned out that it was too good to be true. She, after much agonizing, decided she really wasn't a lesbian after all and just wanted to be friends. I was devastated. I had to choose between losing her from my life entirely or compromising and being friends. I decided to compromise. Because if I know one thing, it is that I will suffer to the same degree I wish things were different. I chose to accept reality and not suffer.

I have always been blessed with a large circle of friend. But in 2002, my three closest friends moved out of the neighborhood. My friend Stanley, who lived a short distance from me, was about to retire and spend part of the year in Florida. It would be a big loss for me, as we had season tickets to the symphony and spent many a Saturday morning having breakfast at Trio's, a neighborhood diner. Judith, who lived across the street and had guided me through many rough parts of my rehabilitation, decided to move to West Virginia. A friend and colleague from our Older Women's League (OWL) days, Brigitte, decided to move to Virginia to, as she put it, buy a garage for her car. She lived a few blocks away, and we often met on Sundays for tea or a walk down to the Smithsonian Museums on The Mall to see some art. My newly ex-lover and these three were the center of my universe, and now it seemed everyone was scattering. I decided to return home to Hawaii.

I returned to Hawaii in March 2003. I worked in a temporary position for the Life Foundation, again hired by a friend. After it ended I submitted a grant proposal to the Susan G. Komen for the Cure Foundation and started the Lesbian Breast Cancer Project in 2007. I joined the board of the Aloha Pride Center, the local LGBT community center, in the fall of 2003 and was elected chair in 2005. Since 2008 I have been self-employed, if you can call it that, working on small projects here and there. I run a counseling business out of my apartment that keeps me in spare change.

My hip has been steadily deteriorating over the years because I have not put my full weight on it. Bones need weight-bearing exercise to stay healthy. So my left hip joint and thigh bone have succumbed to osteoporosis and arthritis, and to avoid a spontaneous break I use my wheelchair full time now. I walked with a walker for several years, but the threat of falling and breaking my leg kept me in the wheelchair. But it was a strategy with a flaw, as I slipped and fell anyway while getting out of a swimming pool in 2008 and broke my leg (tibia). It took a long time to recover. I was in the hospital for eleven days (the Slippery Slope) and essentially in bed for six weeks after that. The Elks Club, where I fell, provided home health aides for me for the entire time. If they hadn't I would have gone to a nursing home.

In 2011 I had an accident with my scooter and broke my hip. I was quite surprised to find that the surgeon suggested repairing it. The previous surgeon had said that I would be in a nursing home for months because there was nothing they could do. But the broken leg three years earlier changed things. Since I now longer beared weight and was in the wheelchair full time, they could put a rod in my hip. I was in the hospital three days instead of months. And after the wound healed, the surgeon said I could stand on it again, and that is what I do now. You never know what the next situation will be.

I have an electric scooter that I use outside on a daily basis. I use my manual wheelchair in the house. I live alone and take care of all my needs myself. I live in a government-subsidized senior high-rise in Honolulu on the twenty-fifth floor overlooking the city, the harbor, and the entire west coast of Oahu down to Barber's Point. The sunsets from my lanai are spectacular. There is a luxury high-rise next door for which the residents paid upward of $700,000 for an apartment like mine. It is very satisfying and ironic that I have the same view for $480 a month.

Moving back home to Hawaii has been a good move for me. The weather is almost always wonderful. The people are almost always wonderful too, and my family is here. My brother, Christopher, is now retired and generously shares his time with me. My niece, Jennifer, has now moved back to Hawaii as well, so I have someone to play with on weekends. It seems now that you can't be my friend unless you have known me at least forty years. I have friends I grew up with, friends I went to school with, and friends I worked with at the Girl Scouts in the seventies. I like being back among my people.

I have found it difficult to make lesbian friends here; I have made a lot of acquaintances through the Lesbian Arts and Culture Exchange (LACE) but no friends like I had in DC. I am not sure exactly why. So I guess my years as a lesbian disability activist are over, and now I am a writer and hanger-out-with-old-friends kind of girl.

I believe that my disability keeps me from making new friends. If you want to be friends with me you will have to always be the one to put my wheelchair in the car, push me up hills, and live through the embarrassment of being with me in public. People will notice and stare or make comments. We might have to rearrange the restaurant or make a fuss about the inaccessible bathroom. It is a pain in the ass to take me places. There is a question a minute. Is the entrance accessible? Can we get my wheelchair between the tables? Is the bathroom accessible? Will they have to help me? What if I pee in my pants? Will they always feel they have to pay for me? And everyone I meet who had a bad experience with a person in a wheelchair, a grumpy old aunt or a grandmother, is likely to be reminded of it and project it on to me. Others approach me like I'm a project: "Look, I have a friend in a wheelchair," just like they might collect a black friend or a Jewish friend. Others are overwhelmed with the logistics; I can't get into their house, so I don't get invited to parties. Bottom line: It is a lot of bother to get to know me.

And if a potential partner pops into view, will they ask themselves, Will I always have to hover to help carry things, reach things? Will I always feel sorry that her life is so hard? Do they feel bad that they just don't want to have to deal with the wheelchair and everything else? Do they realize they will never be the one waited on? That I will never serve them breakfast in bed, clean the house as a surprise, or come pick them up? It is clear we are not equal; we will not share the chores equally, and we will not share equally working in the garden, mowing the lawn, washing the car, carrying in the groceries, or making the beds.

If I do something for a friend they seem embarrassed. Sometimes I worry that I am seen as a pitiful, brave little Margaret struggling to do something nice, like a child trying to make something for Mother. Only with my close friends do I feel somewhat equal; they are used to me and know what I *am* capable of. It has been a struggle to redefine who I am after everything changed.

Chapter 4

Not So Silent Retreat

Seven months after I became disabled, I went with a friend on a seven-day silent Buddhist retreat. Since March, when I became disabled, I had been discharged from the rehabilitation hospital, lived with friends for a few months, and finally moved back into my apartment. I could now stand and walk with a walker. .I could drive using hand controls provided by Vocational Rehabilitation Services, and I was living independently. This was the beginning of the era of "let's find out what we can do now" and of figuring out how I was going to live a meaningful life in a wheelchair.

The retreat, held at a Catholic Monastery in New Jersey, was led by Shinzen Young, an American Buddhist monk trained in Japan who had a successful Vipassana teaching practice in the United States. Nearly one hundred people participated. Once the silence was imposed on the first evening, we were not to utter another word until the closing bell seven days later.

Our days were organized into several sittings a day where we sat on cushions on the floor in silent meditation for forty-five minutes at a time, interspersed with walking meditations, rest periods, meals, and dharma talks. Some of us leaned against the walls, but most sat upright on their cushions. We were decked out a variety of blankets, shawls, and sweatshirts to ward off the chill of sitting still. We staked out our territory and returned to the same cushion for each sitting.

The day started at 5:30 a.m. with chanting and then a silent meditation. Breakfast at 8:00 a.m. was served buffet style in the dining room, as were all the other meals. We ate in silence and were expected to keep our eyes lowered during the meal. We were to take each bite into our mouths and chew slowly, savoring every texture and taste, and set our forks down between bites. Before the next bite, we were to take a breath. The meals were very peaceful. I felt comforted by the pace. There was no hurry to finish and no need to make small talk with strangers.

The sittings were interspersed with walking meditations during which we walked very slowly, attempting to feel our heels hit the floor, then our toes, then the shift of weight, and so on. I walked with my walker in those days, and it struck me as pretty funny that everyone else was now trying to emulate me, for that is how I walked all the time: slowly, watching every step. I could tell you about the carpet pattern on every floor.

Shinzen offered a question and answer period in the late morning for those with questions about their experiences. I always attended, as I wanted a break from the meditation hall. One day someone asked about the experience of "no self," a Buddhist idea that it is our egos, our selves, that think and grasp onto things that cause us to suffer. So to attain no self would remove suffering from our lives. Shinzen talked a bit, and then I asked a question. "How would you know you attained no self if you had no self to experience it? How would you know?" I was rewarded with "good question" praise from the leader. He said you would know afterward that you had attained that state. I have to admit that like most answers from Buddhist teachers it left me wondering.

Shinzen also gave a dharma talk every evening for about an hour, teaching us about Buddhism. The talks were fascinating to me. I had been thirsty a long time, and he was offering me long, cold drinks of water. His words made sense to me. They had a familiar ring to them, as my father was a Zen Buddhist and often gave dharma talks at the dinner table when I was in middle school. I elaborate more on his teachings in the Spirituality chapter. I would be nodding my head, agreeing with point after point Shinzen made. He was a science-oriented fellow who liked to write little formulas on the board. L x R = S: Life times Resistance equals Suffering. Cute but to the point.

From the moment I settled in and closed my eyes in the first meditation, an enormous anger erupted inside me. It burned furiously for days. A friend who accompanied me on the retreat noticed I was having a difficult time and one day left some candies on my mat. This act of kindness infuriated me! Talk about being out of your head! Why would an act of kindness make me so mad? I picked up the candies and threw them across the meditation hall. Luckily no one else was in the hall at the time. After a few minutes I recovered my senses and retrieved them.

When the group reassembled in the hall, I had to leave because I was afraid I would scream out loud. The demons were out in full force for the first time. I wheeled myself up to my room, put the pillow over my face, and screamed and screamed and screamed. My life had been turned upside down, and my beautiful body was broken. I used to run, and now I could barely stand. My income was more than cut in half. . I was in constant pain, and everything, every–god–damned–thing was so hard! The numbness that had set in back in March was wearing off. I was so heavily drugged those first few months that the anger accumulated without my noticing it. But now it was going to have its say. The demons continued yelling in my ear: "What will happen to me now that I'm 'rehabilitated?" I could barely manage in my apartment. It took five months for the first Social Security Disability Insurance (SSDI) check to arrive. I was broke. I could not work full-time. I had just changed careers from community organizing to massage which I could no longer do, so how the hell was I going to earn money now?

I had survived all the indignities, large and small, at the rehab hospital: crapping in my bed when the chaplain arrived, peeing all over my physical therapist (PT) while practicing getting up off the floor, crashing into the curb nine hundred times trying to learn to pop a wheelie, sitting stock-still barely breathing while unimaginable pain swept through my belly, being left sitting on the toilet while the aide wandered off and not being able to do anything about it, and being forced to participate in a so-called therapy group that was beyond stupid.

Before I was disabled, if I wanted to go out for a bite to eat, I decided where to go to, grabbed my keys, and left. But now I had to figure out how I would get there and whether to take the car, the scooter, the wheelchair, or the walker. Was the restaurant accessible? Was there an accessible bathroom? After I arrived at the restaurant, I discovered that I couldn't get between the tables, and it turned into a big !@#$%^&* deal to rearrange the place so I could get in. People had to stand up and interrupt their meals so I could roll to my table. Once at the table there was another !@#$%^& discussion and decision about where I would sit, with the waiters taking the chairs away and putting them back until we finally decided. Or if I transferred into one of their chairs, there was another big discussion about where to store the wheelchair. On and on and on. No more walking to the corner restaurant, sliding into a booth, and having a peaceful meal. Everything was now a big-ass production.

Life as I knew it was down the toilet. I was single. Who would want a partner in a wheelchair? I was in pain, unrelenting pain, and there didn't seem to be any relief in sight. What in !@#$%^&* hell was going to happen to me? I screamed and screamed. And then I sobbed.

I was bereft…bereft. A deep sorrow consumed me right down to the bone. After a time I grew calm. I sat there in my little room, attempting to breathe in and out. Slowly a little of my Buddhist practice started to seep in.

"Who exactly is suffering here?" I asked myself. Why was I so desperate to hold on to my previous life? People had lives in wheelchairs. People did actually survive on the amount of money SSDI gave me. I could find other work to do. The pain couldn't last forever. When I began to let go of what used to be and began to embrace what was, I felt better. The sorrow cranked down a notch.

I returned to the meditation hall and took my place on my cushion. I looked all around me at the silent figures appearing like geologic formations in Canyonland, wrapped in shawls, faces serene. There was a faint hint of incense in the air. A flower garden was visible through the window. Dust motes were illuminated in the air around the little altar in the front of the room. There were faint sounds from the kitchen a floor below us. The gong struck to mark the end of the session reverberated endlessly to a quiet whisper.

While sitting in the garden a short while later, I was aware of a breeze caressing one side of my face and not the other. My right shoulder was warmer from the sun than my left. There were faint traffic sounds from the distant freeway. I tried to name the myriad of colors in the hedges both near and far. A dragonfly flitted by, pausing here and there. I was amazed to see that it had two sets of gossamer wings I had never noticed before. Every nerve fiber in my body was alive and welcomed every sensation with open arms.

The last two days of the retreat were calm, my mediations deep. I left there as if floating on air. I couldn't imagine why anyone ever bothered talking; it seemed so unnecessary. A great peace now dwelled within me. The sorrow had dissipated. I knew then I was going to survive.

Chapter 5

The Study of Sex

In 1999 I participated in a research study looking at the sexuality of women who had suffered spinal cord injuries. I was a little older and a little less heterosexual than the researchers wanted, but I think they were desperate for participants. I was to be paid $500 to go to Kessler Rehabilitation Hospital in New Jersey for several days to participate in the study.

I was still in my "let's find out about my new self" phase and eager to participate. In order for the study to be considered valid, the researcher had to conduct a study of women the same way studies for men had been conducted. Or at least that is what I supposed they were doing by showing us pornographic videos and having us stimulate ourselves with a vibrator. It didn't exactly sound like a study designed to examine women's sexuality. Men, so they tell us, are object oriented. Things like pornography appeal to them because there are objects, not real people, to relate to. Women, being from Venus, are relational. The relationship is more important than anything else. So why would watching couples having sex be arousing to women? If you really wanted to study women's sexuality you would have to bring their partners along with them to see how they related to them. But scientific research is dominated by men, and to be accepted into their realm I suppose the researchers had to go along with the male model for the study.

I told the woman running the study that I was a lesbian and would like to see lesbian pornography instead of straight porn. I knew full well that I was sending her on mission impossible. To my knowledge there is no true lesbian porn out there. My community has been wishing for it for years! Lesbians are just not into what the mainstream heterosexual community and gay men think of as pornographic. When we do make an erotic film about lesbians, it is usually all about love, not sex.

The woman was very pleased with herself for finding what she thought was lesbian porn. Sure enough, there were two or three nearly naked women fondling each other. Nearly naked in that they were wearing six-inch heels and jewelry and lots of makeup. They had long salon-styled hair and breasts that looked like melon halves stuck under the skin of their chests. Their breasts didn't wiggle or jiggle a bit. They never smiled, nor did they look like they were enjoying themselves. They kissed, they fondled and licked each other, and I had a hard time keeping from laughing right out loud. This male fantasy was light years away from lesbian sex as I had experienced it.

But they were paying me $500, so I let them hook me up to a device that measures blood flow in the vagina and some other device that measures muscle contractions. I watched the videos and applied a variety of vibrators. Never mind that I had no feeling whatsoever in my groin. I felt a bit detached, like I was doing something to someone else.

This went on for three days when they finally sat me down and explained that I was functioning normally physiologically. I had enough blood flow and nerve stimulation to achieve an orgasm, but it would take something like twenty minutes of stimulation. Well, I don't know about you, but diddling myself for twenty minutes to achieve an orgasm I couldn't feel didn't exactly sound like fun to me. I told this to a straight friend when I got home, and she said, well, then you can still have sex…thereby, I think, revealing more about her sex life than she meant to. I was a lesbian; I was not inclined to have sex if I couldn't feel it. A straight girl might be willing to lie there and let a man have sex on/in/with her, but why would any self-respecting lesbian participate in something like that? I came to find out, though, that sex is really in your head.

This is a good thing. Tactile stimulation of my groin results in jangled nerve sensations, like stepping on your foot when it has gone to sleep. It hurts, but not in a bad way. I suspect the S&M folks would understand what I mean. And the parts that don't jangle are numb.

I believe that men with spinal cord injuries, given the choice to walk again or have an erection, would choose the latter. They are obsessed with the topic. Me, I don't care too much either way, as sex has not been a driving force in my life. In addition to having a somewhat numb crotch, I had a double mastectomy in 2005, which denied me yet another of the usual avenues of sexual arousal.

I have had sex since the onset of my disability, and I can tell you now with great certainty that it is truly in your head. I like having sex. It feels good to be intimate with someone. I like snuggling in bed next to a nude body. I think I am a better lover than I was before. I can totally rejoice in my partner's pleasure and not be distracted by my needs. With just a little effort I can vividly remember what it felt like to have an orgasm of my own. Squeezing my lover's nipples also zaps my memory circuits. Thank goodness I have forty years of sexual memory to call on.

Strangely enough, all of my senses are enhanced now: touch, sound, smell, taste, and the sight of things now move me in ways they did not before. Wonderful sensual memories are stimulated when I watch someone dance, walk along the beach, or body surf. With a little effort I can recall in a sumptuous symphony of sensation the feel of the water, the sand under my feet, and my muscles rejoicing in the sheer joy of moving. As nice as that is, though, part of me misses the real thing.

Chapter 6

Pain and Suffering

I am in constant pain. The pain in my legs is unrelenting, present every minute of every day since March 1, 1997. I have neuropathic pain from my waist to my toes from the nerves that were damaged by the bleeding blood vessel and a left hip joint that is deteriorating from arthritis. My broken hip has been repaired, but there is no effective treatment for the elimination of neuropathic pain that I know of.

My pain has several layers. The bass line is a tingling, burning sensation. It modulates. Sometimes it is so intense that I would not be surprised to see that my legs are charred stumps. Other times it just a maddening tingle, like a foot gone to sleep. On occasion, at night, I have twitchy spasms in my right calf and ankle that cause my toes to contract and then splay out in a sharp, painful irregular rhythm. If I sit up in my wheelchair for several hours a sharp pain radiates from my hip up the left side of my back. Some days it feels like I am sitting on a hot, lumpy brick with an intense burning sensation and pressure in my groin.

On the days when I succumb to it, the constant pain exhausts me mentally, physically, and spiritually. I can't concentrate. I can't sleep well, tossing and turning all night trying to get comfortable. I wake up wishing I had died in the night. It takes a few minutes to shake off the feeling and get right with the world. There are days when I melt down and just can't take it another minute. But here I am yet another day, still here, still in pain.

But on a good day, I choose not to suffer. Pain and suffering are usually thought of as one and the same, but they are not. Pain is a physical *sensation* to which we assign the *feeling* of suffering. The sensation is real enough, but it actually has no inherent value assigned to it. We have the choice to assign the value, and most of us choose to label it suffering. Suffering is just a thought though, not a tangible reality. It is a thought the same as when I think I will have a tuna sandwich instead of ham, or I think I will put mayonnaise instead of mustard on my sandwich. It is all in the mind. Just as ham is not inherently better than tuna, we make a judgment that it is. I have pain, but I do not suffer like you might think I would under the circumstances.

Western medicine doctors have only a few weapons in their pain treatment arsenal. First, in the rehab hospital they gave me time-release morphine. It controlled the pain very well, but I was living on another planet. I made a tape recording during that time and was horrified later to hear how I slurred my words and grasped for a train of thought. At the time I thought I was right on top of things. The experience gave me a much better understanding of drug addicts. But this wasn't how I wanted to live my life.

The doctors assured me that I would not become addicted. I took the time-release morphine for nine months, and when we started to reduce the dose, I felt miserable. The doctor told me I was habituated, not addicted, but really what's the difference? So I went to my acupuncturist, who taped a BB in my ear and told me to squeeze it to activate the pressure point in my ear when I felt bad. It worked quite well.

After I was unhabituated from the morphine, I was given in succession over the next few years the rest of the drugs in the neuropathic pain arsenal. First was Elavil, which left me very spacey, and I gained thirty pounds in the first month, which I have never been able to shake off. I complained about feeling spacey all the time, and we switched to Neurontin, which at the smallest therapeutic dose left me so doped up that I could not function as a normal adult. The last attempt was Lyrica, which also left me very sleepy, and it cost forty dollars a month, which I could not afford.

In 2001 I finally had a doctor who listened to me about how unacceptable it was to be drugged all the time. She installed a Medtronic intrathecal pump in my abdomen. The pump is a small tuna-fish-can-sized object that rests just under my skin in my abdomen. It has a catheter wrapped around my side under the skin that delivers one-three-hundredth of the dose of the drugs I was taking orally directly into my spinal fluid. The drugs sink directly into my legs and do not circulate through my brain or liver. I am now awake, and the pain is reduced to tolerable levels.

The drugs in the pump allow me to exercise easier too, which is a win-win situation. I feel better when I exercise, but the pain and sleepiness were preventing me from exercising as much as I should have. By the time the doctor prescribed the pump, my legs were getting rigid, and the muscle relaxant Baclofen was the first drug put in my pump. It was also thought that if we reduced the spasms and rigidity that the pain would reduce as well. Turns out it was correct. I now have a cocktail of Baclofen and morphine.

In 2004 I went into treatment with Dr. Anna Li, a Chinese-trained acupuncturist and Western-trained medical doctor. She treated me with very large needles in my head, which hurt like hell, but my left leg, which had been hanging there for years rather uselessly, woke up. I now had a slight sensation in the dermatome (the pattern your nerves follow down your leg) and on the bottom of my foot. She joked and said we should go to China where she could really fix me up. I understand that China, without the Religious Right's restrictions on stem cell research, is forging ahead and making great progress treating spinal cord injuries like mine. I would love to see what could be done with both Eastern and Western medicine working together. Acupuncture helps me maintain my balance physically and spiritually in ways I cannot explain. There are many acupuncturists working in the U.S. now, and I recommend the treatment highly. Insurance usually won't pay for it, but if you can afford it, it is worth it.

I think the pump treatment is headed in the right direction. But it is just a start. Because we are mind/body creatures, just dealing with the physical pain is not enough. Pain has many elements. In addition to the physical sensations, there are very real psychological and spiritual elements.

If it was possible to measure pain empirically, and you asked two people with the same level of pain about their experiences, the stories would be very different. Pain itself is actually not definable. We feel a sensation, and we label it pain. But why, for instance, does one woman with a migraine stagger into bed for three days while another manages to get dinner on the table? Why is it when a man smashes his thumb with the hammer, he swears and sucks it up, while a child who does the same thing screams for fifteen minutes? One could assume they had the same level of pain, so why the different reactions?

I am coming to understand that my experience of pain is based on my story about pain. We all have a story about pain; our sex, gender, culture, family systems, and more have all given us this story. Our parents taught us at a very young age how to suffer, how to deal with difficulties, how to react to stressful situations, and this leads us to experience pain differently. Men are taught to suppress their reactions to pain, and children are allowed to express their pain. If when you were young one of your parents went to bed with something as simple as a hangnail, you learned from them what a person is supposed to do when they have pain, any level of pain, and you will do the same thing as an adult. If on the other hand your parents were stoic about pain that is what you will most likely do when you have any level of pain. It is a learned response. A good example of how expectations dictate behavior is fainting in Victorian society. Upper-class white women were expected to faint, get the vapors, at anything distasteful, like the sight of blood, upon hearing tragic news. Well, upper-class white women are still seeing blood, hearing tragic news, but they no longer faint. Fainting was a learned behavior, just like we learn to suffer from pain.

When I get distracted I forget about my pain. Why does distraction work as well as a drug? All the drugs given me are also prescribed in larger doses for depression, so why do the same drugs work for psychic pain and physical pain? I think Western medicine's approach is too narrow. It is in the mind, not the brain, where pain is experienced. The mind is influenced by hundreds of things in determining a response to pain. Yet Western medicine offers only drugs to dull it. I venture to say they are looking in all the wrong places. The experience of pain, it seems to me, is mostly psychological, not physiological. It is true that your body does react physically to pain by pulling your hand back from burning object, but the experience of pain is all in your mind.

I believe we were also taught how to manage life crises. If you were a person who dealt with things in a straightforward manner before horrible things happened to you, I suspect that you will deal with your situation in the same manner. If, however, you were a person who blamed others for your plight, avoided taking responsibility, and took to your bed with a little headache, then that is how you will approach your altered state. If you see life as a half-empty glass, unfair and cruel, you will suffer magnificently. But if you see life as the half-full glass you will suffer less.

I choose not to suffer. Byron Katie says in her book, *A Thousand Names for Joy*, that you will suffer to the same degree you wish things were different. Absolutely! I am here to testify, to witness, to swear on a stack of Bibles, that that is the truth for me. On a good day when I am present to what is, my experience of pain is less and my life worth living. On a day when life seems overwhelming, together the thoughts nearly kill me. The only difference between these two days is my thinking. My empirical level of pain is probably the same. On the days I suffer, enormous bags of garbage roar out of my psyche and beat me up. Why me? What did I do to deserve this? I can't believe I am so miserable and still alive. This is so fucking unfair. What did I do to cause this? Soon I am sitting in a puddle of misery.

On a day when I choose not to suffer, I experience my pain as an interesting sensation and my life as a fascinating challenge, no judgment attached. I just notice. I breathe. I sit in meditation.

I say the Buddhist heart sutra, *metta*, to myself: I desire myself freedom from suffering. I desire myself happiness. I desire myself health. And it comes true. I sit in gratitude for all the blessings that have come my way.

Some days when the sensation is really intense, I do a guided meditation by Shinzen Young on his tape called *Break Through Pain* (available at www.soundstrue.com). The mediation allows me to take a step back and observe the sensation instead of wallowing in it. Following his instructions, I first take my awareness around the outside of my pain. What shape is it? Is it round, smooth, or does it have sharp edges? I sit with that for a while and then take my awareness inside the pain. Is it thick, thin, watery, or viscous? I sit with that for a while and then take my awareness to the rest of my body and check in with it. Am I tense, holding my breath, furrowing my brow, or clenching my fist? I relax every part of me, let my belly soften, and breathe in and out easily. The last part of the mediation is to extend my awareness to everything all at once, outside the sensation, inside the sensation, in my body and now outside my body, in the room and out into the universe. I feel so very serene, very connected to everything everywhere from the beginning of time to the end of time, and then finally to no thought at all. Just a peaceful, calm, whiteness. I cherish those moments. I don't always get to that place, nor is it a goal. If it happens, it happens. Some days I barely start sitting, and all sorts of other things pop into my mind and won't get out. On those days I have the privilege to notice what is distracting me.

In the many years I have been treated for chronic pain, until recently not one doctor offered a referral to psychotherapy to help me cope or referred me to a wellness clinic to learn about mind/body healing techniques or to an acupuncturist trained with a 4,000-year history of successfully treating pain. No one mentioned massage. Not one ever suggested that meditation might help. Not one of them has ever talked to me about what this pain means to me in my life. My whole body and soul hurt, but the doctor's only solution was to prescribe drugs to dull the senses. What if I want to be awake?

I recently went to a pain clinic at my HMO. I am encouraged that they offer a six-week course on managing pain, which includes the mind/body connection, nutrition, physical therapy, adopting healthy attitudes, and the like. My physician seems to have the same understanding of the experience of pain that I have. I am more encouraged than I have been in years that together we will find a way to better manage my pain.

Chapter 7

Slippery Slope

In June 2008 I slipped at the Elks Club swimming pool and shattered the head of my left tibia (lower leg). I spent the next eleven days in the hospital and the next two months in bed, and a year later I still could not stand on it. It felt like I had gone two steps forward and one back; I did not return to the same level of mobility that I enjoyed before the fall. This incident with my leg left me pondering the slippery slope of aging as a person with a disability.

It feels like my disability has made me old before my time. The aging time line has sped up, for I now have problems in my early sixties that I thought I would not have to deal with until much later in life. Of course, we really never know what the future will bring, and expectations often make us miserable when things turn out differently than we expected. But I have noticed a few things.

The hospital assigned me to the skilled nursing ward, where all the other patients were very elderly and, to be honest, decrepit. As

I wandered the halls, it was like a visit from the ghost of Christmas future. At times I feel I live in an eighty-year-old body. At sixty-five with a spinal cord injury I am already incontinent, have severe mobility limitations, experience pain 24-7, and live on a fixed income, and now I have moved into senior housing. Most sixty-five-year-olds are not dealing with these things. I dread to think what will happen as I age over the next 10 or 20 years and my body becomes 105. Yikes! My so-called golden years have a dark lining.

My broken leg gave me a scary taste of the future. Before the break I was normally quite independent. I went out each day in my scooter to events, lunches, to do my own shopping. But with my leg in a cast I could not get into my bathroom or kitchen or onto my scooter. I was dependent on home health aides provided by the Elks Club to empty my pee bucket, feed me, wash me, and fetch all sorts of thing that were out of my reach. It was clear that if something permanent like this happened to me, this would become my daily routine. My lack of mobility isolated me. I became dependent on friends stopping by to see me and had to wait until they had time in their schedules. I could no longer get on my scooter and go to the club for lunch or go shopping. If I wanted something from the store I had to wait until someone could go get it, and worse, I had to ask for every little thing. No independence.

I am surrounded daily with reminders of what the hazards of old age do to a person here in senior housing. Lunch is served here five days a week by Meals on Wheels, and about sixty of the residents participate. Most can't walk well, so there is quite a collection of canes, walkers, and wheelchairs in the room. Some are alert and some are not. Some of the other residents sit on the bench outside the front door all day with nothing to do. A crowd collects in the lobby if the mail is late. Those in this frail crowd do not fit the image I have of myself. Yet here I am.

I went on Social Security at age fifty-two, at least ten years before anyone else I knew. My plan was to work into my late sixties or early seventies, but my disability took me out of the workforce fifteen years sooner than I expected, right when I was earning my peak salary. When I turned fifty I realized that I had little in retirement savings and started a vigorous plan because I was then earning more than I had ever earned before. But my disability cut that plan short. I thought I would supplement my Social Security for ten years or so, putting me well into my seventies before I ran out of money…and who knew if I would even live that long? But here I am in my early sixties, and I have already run through my savings. Social Security Disability Insurance covers only the very basics of my monthly expenses, and if I do not have a part-time job, I have to dip into my savings. If I am not working, and my expenses exceed my income as they often do, the difference goes on my credit card, with the hope that I can pay it off when I get another job. I dread to think about what will happen when I can no longer work.

I feel like I have slipped down a notch on the slippery slope. Not so long ago I lived in a lovely Victorian three-bedroom house, and now I live in a government-subsidized studio. Not so long ago I earned $50,000 a year, and now SSDI provides me $15,000 a year. Not long ago no one looked over my shoulder; now SSA tells me how much I can earn, an inaccessible world limits my mobility, and the senior residence has six single-spaced pages of rules. I have control over very little now, except, of course, how I feel about it!

Before my spinal cord injury, I was living the good life. I thought I was making a difference in the world. I was working in the national offices of women's organizations in Washington, DC. I sat on the boards of directors for cutting-edge agencies. I had very interesting friends. I traveled. I lived in Dupont Circle, in the heart of Washington, and loved it. I was a tall, athletic lesbian who loved to dance. But then in a serendipitous moment a blood vessel burst in my spinal cord, and I got old all of a sudden.

I now work at part-time jobs when I can find them. They are usually temporary little jobs. I rarely get to use my expertise anymore, as most of the jobs are clerical. I no longer sit on any boards. I can't afford to go on trips. I find myself, however, in a strange conundrum where I don't want to live that life anymore, yet I miss it. After years of being in the thick of things, I now no longer read the paper or watch the news. I just don't care anymore about global warming, the economy, or saving the whales. My world has shrunk down to the realm of self-interest. I only want to know now if the pool will be closed or if I am going to get a cost-of-living increase to my check.

I spent forty-five years in the trenches battling every sort of injustice, and it is now strange to not care. Let the young people who will have to live with pollution, corrupt governments, and wobbly economies get out there and do something about it. I protested all my life, participated in a dozen marches on Washington, wrote my congressperson regularly, attended endless meetings, and what did it get me? Women still earn seventy-five cents on the dollar to men. Gay men and lesbians still cannot marry. We are still marching off to ridiculous wars in the name of patriotism (not to mention the elimination of weapons of mass destruction). Cars are not that much safer. We are still dependent on foreign oil. We are still the most obese nation in the world. Young girls dress like prostitutes on the prowl because of advertising. Young girls are still getting pregnant in droves. The Pope is still an idiot. Black men are still being pulled over by racial profiling. The majority of restaurants in Hawaii still have inaccessible bathrooms. And I am tired of it all.

My elderly experience also includes hiring someone to clean my house because I can't do it. In addition, I get all the special considerations the elderly receive with the commiserate loss of independence. People often open doors for me, fetch my food at a buffet, bring my food to the table at the fast food restaurants, or take me to appointments in their car. I know this sounds like a silly complaint, but how would you feel if everyone helped you at every turn? On the up side, I have claimed the senior discount everywhere for years. Who is going to challenge an old lady in a wheelchair? In fact, I finagle everywhere I can to get a discount. I hate doing it, but I just cannot afford to pay full fare for hardly anything. My friends and family are very good about paying for my meals, and one friend even gave me her extra frequent flyer miles for a trip. I am grateful for their support, but deep down inside somebody is very embarrassed and ashamed. Some little voice protests, saying you should be taking care of yourself, this is charity, and charity is for those who can't take care of themselves. Luckily it is a very quiet voice, and I can shut it off easily.

Don't get me wrong; I am not sitting around waiting for the other shoe to drop. Most days I am happy, content, and appreciative of the delicious irony of it all. I am just acknowledging the slope. I know that staying present, dealing with reality instead of wishing things were different, will help keep me from Codgerville. I do call Handi-Van and get out. I swallow my pride and make the call to my friends to do things for me. The Buddhists teach us that dependence and independence are just different sides of the same coin. Maybe so.

In my darkest moments, I wonder now in my sixty-fifth year if the best part of my life is over. Do I have anything but pain and poverty to look forward to in the future? The good old days seem all in the past, and the future looks grim. I understand much better now an old geezer sitting on a park bench repeating his World War II experiences over and over. When did the worm turn? When did the past become more interesting than the possibility of the future or even what is happening today?

I have a life now. It's just not the life I used to have, and it sure is not the life I thought I was going to have. Demons whisper in my ear in the dark of night. I don't drive anymore, and I wonder how long I will be able to get along with my scooter. Will I become more disabled as time goes by? Will I get diabetes like my father and brother? Will my osteopenia turn into osteoporosis? Look what happened, the whisper goes, when I broke my leg, it incapacitated me for nearly six months. What will happen when the arthritis in my hands gets so bad that it prevents me from manually assisting my bowel movements? My blood pressure is on the rise; what if I have a stroke on top of my spinal cord injury? I manage limited exercise now—what happens when I can't?

Facing all this is tough. But I have survived so far, and realistically there is no reason to assume that I won't continue to survive. I ask these questions with hopefully a clear mind, a bright eye, and a sense of wonder. I don't sit home alone pining away. I am a cheerful person most of the time. I know I will suffer in direct proportion to how much I wish things were different. I live in Hawaii, one of the most beautiful places on earth, and each morning I get to look out over the harbor and Honolulu. Rainbows appear almost every morning. I meditate every day to calm my spirit and remind myself that I am connected. But in the middle of the night sometimes I wonder, like the line from that old Peggy Lee song, "Is that all there is?"

Chapter 8

Ignorant and Arrogant in Italy

In 2001 I took a trip to Italy, my first trip outside the U.S. since attaining my altered state. I was going to visit a friend, Renata, who lived in Milan. Two friends from massage school spoke up and said they would be happy to push me around Italy.

Italy is a wonderful place to visit. But my friends and I were clueless as to how an inaccessible country could change me from an independent person with a disability into a helpless cripple! We all meant well, but we didn't get it. Without having experienced a foreign country in a wheelchair I didn't know what questions to ask, nor did I know what I would need. I was clueless about how to be handicapped, and I felt truly handicapped by Italy.

Upon my arrival at the Milan airport I attempted to call Renata and tell her I had arrived safely. I was by myself as my friends were coming in the next day. I could not reach the phone in the phone booth. The phones in Italy have a digital display giving instructions about when to insert the money. I asked a woman at the information desk to help, and she was very dismissive, like what kind of idiot needs help using the phone. I explained that I could not see the phone, and she finally agreed to help.

It also became obvious that I could not use the train to get to Milan as suggested by my hostess, because there was no way to get my bags from baggage claim to the train. I had thought I could get a skycap to do it, but no. So I wound up taking a taxi to Renata's house for ninety dollars instead of the ten-dollar train.

On our first day in Milan, we set out to see the Duomo after being assured that the subway was accessible. Well, sort of. There was a chairlift that descended a hundred yards down into the subway. It was locked. We finally located the key and set off on the scariest ride of my life. On the way home, however, we made a mad dash for the escalator, and amidst much yelling from the subway attendant to stop, we ascended by hanging on to the handrails. It somehow seemed safer than the lift!

While at the Piazza del Duomo I went into the Museo del Duomo to ask if I could use the bathroom. My question prompted a loud, hand-waving discussion between the guards and ticket sellers, who finally agreed that I had to purchase a ticket. I had exhausted my phrase-book Italian with the first question and now was completely out of the picture. Finally, they directed me to a public toilet across the Piazza. So we set off across the very scenic cobblestone Piazza. *Bump, bump, bumpity, bump, bump;* we arrived at a locked handicap bathroom. We finally found the attendant, who I am pretty sure said he did not have the key and we should go back across the Piazza to the shopping galleria. So off we went: *bump, bump, bumpity, bump, bump* across the Piazza and finally arrived at an accessible bathroom. It had been forty-five minutes since I had first asked at the museum, and I was now sitting in a puddle.

Our next stop was Venice. Did you know that all those bridges in Venice are covered in stairs? There are quaint cobblestone side-walks and a stair-covered bridge every two hundred yards in that beautiful city. My friends became expert in bumping me up and down steps. We also became expert in transferring into a gondola bouncing at the dock. By the time we returned to the train station we were looking forward to a quiet ride back to Milan.

The train was due to leave at 8:00 p.m. At 7:59 the lift had not arrived, so I pulled myself up with my arms into the car, much to the amazement of the three conductors standing by. I was a fifty-seven-year-old gray-haired woman boosting herself into the train car. Their expressions were priceless.

But the fun was only beginning. When we arrived in Milan a lift was waiting at the doorway. After I got on the lift, the attendant lowered it, raised the side rails, and attached it to a small tractor. He asked if I wanted a taxi, and I said yes. He cranked up the tractor and took off careening through the train station, dodging pedestrians left and right. My friends were sprinting along behind, desperately trying to keep up. I felt like something out of *Les Miserables* when the prisoners are paraded through the streets! We arrived at the taxi stand, where the driver was quite pleased with himself to have beaten all the other passengers to the taxis. It was few minutes before I could catch my breath to speak.

And don't ask me what we were thinking when we decided to visit Cinque Terre, those quaint little villages perched on the cliffs over the Mediterranean. There are ten million stairs in the most inaccessible, steepest villages in the world. But many young men visit Italy in the summer from all over Europe, and if asked by an old lady in a wheelchair they are most willing to help out. With the help of two of those strong young men I even went swimming in the Mediterranean off the ferry dock. I dove off the dock, and two handsome German men pulled me in like a fisherman's net. The water looked so wonderful, so blue and refreshing that I could not resist.

But by the time we reached Rome a week later my friends had had it. They went on a side trip to Naples, leaving me alone in the hotel. The hotel was located on a very busy cobblestone street with no sidewalk. You had to step out the front door directly into to the street. I was essentially a prisoner in the hotel. I sat in my room all day crying, exhausted from the previous two weeks of trying to deal with a hostile environment. Inaccessible Italy with its eighteen-inch curbs, cobblestones, and no curb cuts had defeated me, and I decided to go home.

I checked into the airport Hilton and was immediately transported back to my independent self. The room was accessible, and there were no stairs anywhere in the hotel or airport. In the morning a bellman pushed me over to the Disability Lounge, a separate room where disabled passengers could wait for their flights. A charming young woman offered me a cup of coffee, changed my ticket, checked my bag, and arranged for me to be pushed to the gate in time for my flight.

Realizing the limits of my disability came as a big shock to me. I lived at the time in Washington, DC, and I was lulled into thinking that I was not particularly handicapped. I had an electric scooter, a manual wheelchair, and a walker. I was rarely prevented from going anywhere I wanted to go by using the subway or the buses or just rolling over land. I was independent.

Before leaving home I had not been aware to what extent an accessible environment contributed to my self-image. I felt bad in Italy. I was dependent on my friends for the slightest thing outside my hotel room. I disliked being pushed everywhere. I started resenting my dear, sweet friends because I was so dependent on them, and, vice versa, they started to resent me for being a burden. I felt vulnerable and powerless.

What was I trying to prove with all those acts of derring-do? It was as if somehow doing the impossible made me less crippled, vulnerable, or powerless. But at what point did my identity get tied up with my body image? At home, I felt a keen separation from my body and the whatever-it-is that makes me me. But in Italy that separation merged, and I became my crippled body. An inaccessible environment changed my self-image.

There is an accessible Italy; I just didn't bother to find out. Ignorance and arrogance are a dangerous combination. I was ignorant about the limits of my disability. I thought I was independent when it was actually my environment that allowed me to be independent. Who knew? The thought that I could just pick up and go to a foreign country without doing proper research was just plain arrogant, and I paid a price for it.

My experience with the wheelchair aside, I loved Italy. I loved the food, the people, and the scenery. But the next time I go I will stay in accessible hotels, avail myself of accessible tours, and hire a strong young Italian to push me around. I will let go of the thought of me as a young woman with a backpack and Eurail pass. The reality is I am an elderly disabled woman in a wheelchair who needs a few accommodations to be comfortable.

Chapter 9

The Morning of September 11

On the morning of September 11, 2001, I was in the waiting room of my dentist's office in Washington, DC, about four blocks from the White House. The first I knew anything was amiss was when my dentist dashed out the door with her purse under her arm muttering something about her children. The office staff then invited me to join them to watch the two planes crash into the World Trade Center on the small television in the office. It was horrifying to see the crashes over and over and wonder how many people were being killed. More than three thousand, it turned out later.

When I left the office a few minutes later on my electric scooter, a fourth plane was still in the air and assumed to be headed for the White House. It never made it there because it crashed in Ohio someplace, but I didn't know that at the time. I could see the smoke across the Potomac from where the third plane had crashed into the Pentagon. My usual route home took me right next to the

White House, so I decided to take a different one that kept me a safe distance away.

I felt confused and upset in a strangely vague way. On one hand I was incredulous and disbelieving that this could be happening. On the other I could see the smoke over the Pentagon, which made it seem real enough.

On the way home I stopped in the 7-Eleven and purchased a large bag of Cheetos and two bottles of root beer. These are not things I usually eat, but my inner child steered my scooter right into the store. I needed comfort. I got home, ate all the Cheetos, and drank the root beer while glued to the television. But I needed to do something more.

A friend in Baltimore called and encouraged me to come to her house. In a very short time after the incidents all transportation shut down; all buses, trains, and planes were grounded. I heard on the news that the highways were parking lots, so even if you had a car you had difficulty getting out of DC.

I couldn't get out of town, but the need to do something was strong. I scooted down to St. Matthew's Cathedral, a large Byzantine-style cathedral in the center of DC. The accessible entrance was locked. So I parked my scooter in the alley near a side door, and with the help of two passersby I staggered a few steps into the Cathedral. A number of people had the same idea as

I did, as they sat praying in that beautiful church. The old church was dark and cool; it smelled of incense, old wood, and candles. The pew creaked as I sat down. The seat of the pew was polished brightly by the thousands of bottoms of those who had sat there previously. Candles were lit everywhere, red glass holders aglow in racks by the altar. The altar looked ancient and holy. I am not a Catholic, but this seemed like the place to be, somewhere God might be hanging out. Somewhere where some sense of what had happened might be offered. I prayed for the people who had died, the terrorists who had planned such a horror, the officials trying to deal with the aftermath. Prayer seemed to be the thing to do.

I returned to St. Matthew's the next day for a mass conducted by the Cardinal of DC. I guess he couldn't get out of town either. The accessible entrance to St. Matthew's was now open and led me to the front part of the church near the altar. A number of priests were gathered there. There didn't seem to be any way to get me into the sanctuary, so they invited me to sit with them off to the side. As a Buddhist it was fascinating to see the ancient Mass ritual up close; there is a lot going on that you don't see from the sanctuary. The Cardinal gave a very heartfelt and insightful homily. When it came time for communion, all the priests were busy serving the very large crowd down in the sanctuary, so the Cardinal himself served me communion, as we were the only two left up on the altar. I am sure he would have choked if he knew he was serving Christ's body to a lesbian Buddhist, but I took the wafer in the spirit it was offered.

In the ensuing years since 9/11, I have become convinced that if I am in a building that is attacked or set on fire I will die there. I am not the least convinced that we have adequate plans or the proper equipment to get me and my wheelchair out of a disaster. I heard stories about two people in wheelchairs being rescued on 9/11, but my guess is the rest in wheelchairs were either not helped and abandoned by their colleagues or died with the others unable to get out. Before 9/11 Stanley and I had season tickets to the National Symphony at the Kennedy Center. Our seats were on the third floor, but after 9/11 they would not allow us up there and exchanged our seats for the orchestra level. Stan thought it was great to be moved to better seats. I felt better too; I thought I might have a chance to get out if something happened!

I take two or three plane trips a year. I can't walk, and I have my doubts that the flight crew (who more and more seem to be older women) would be able to carry me to the emergency slide. Disabled persons are prohibited from sitting in the emergency access aisle, but I contend that is the only aisle where I have a chance of getting out of the plane. I could crawl to the slide and take my chances at the bottom and be flattened by the other passengers as they disembark!

Here in Honolulu at the Blaisdell Concert Hall they park the wheelchairs at the ends of the aisles in an attempt to provide handicap seating. The hall is equipped with side aisles only; there is no center aisle and no break in the seating from the front to the rear. I was there one day for a very popular concert, and there was a wheelchair parked at the end of every other aisle down both sides of the hall. In an emergency evacuation the wheelchairs would be trampled by the people trying to get out of the rows. I am surprised the Fire Marshall allows such an arrangement.

I now live on the twenty-fifth floor of an apartment building. I have no expectation of getting out alive if there is a big fire in the building. I don't know how rescue personnel would be able to rescue the twenty-plus people using wheelchairs who live in the building. I was instructed by a fireman once during a drill to go to the stairwell, call the fire department on my cell phone, and wait in my wheelchair for the firemen to come. He said if the stairway doors were kept shut I could be safe there for three hours or so. But all the stairway doors in my building are kept open on a regular basis for ventilation. There are no emergency wheelchairs in the stairwell and not enough staff in the building to take me down in one if one was available. I still think I'd be toast in short order.

So what to do? Make a big stink? Take my chances with the probability that nothing will ever happen? Make peace with my maker now, in case I don't have time later? Or maybe be like Scarlett in Gone with the Wind I will think about it tomorrow.

Chapter 10

I Am No Longer Afraid to Die

My breast cancer recurred in December 2005, and I underwent a double mastectomy. The first occurrence was ten years earlier in 1995. At that time I opted for a lumpectomy and radiation and a full spectrum of alternative healing modalities. I think of cancer as a chronic disease and thought my treatment successful, as I had gone ten years without a recurrence.

In 1995 I started my treatment with a healing ceremony the night before surgery led by Reverend Margee Iddings. On the day of the operation, four clergy friends gathered by my bed in the pre-op room, but the nurse was unimpressed and threw them out. After my surgery the Re-evaluation Counseling community gathered in close to me and provided daily one-way counseling for a month. A friend came over every morning and walked across Sligo Creek Park with me to my radiation sessions. I danced to flamenco music every day in the kitchen while making breakfast. I had acupuncture and massage once a week. I consulted a nutritionist and had started on a vigorous vitamin therapy to take care of the effects of anesthesia. All went well for ten years, and then the lump recurred in the same spot. It was the same cancer and the same size tumor (very small, less than one centimeter).

After she removed my breasts, the surgeon insisted that I stay overnight in the hospital. For most patients a double mastectomy is an outpatient procedure, unbelievable as that may seem. But since my legs are paralyzed, I had to be fitted with pneumatic compression sleeves on my legs that inflate off and on to prevent blood clots. I had told the surgeon before surgery I usually did not need pain meds after surgery, but I woke up to find a morphine drip in my arm. In combination with the anesthesia it made me nauseous, so they kept me a second day. And off we went down the slippery slope of medical care, where they give one drug after another to counteract the side effects of the first drug, whereas in my way to thinking it is better not to start and is exactly why I told the surgeon not to give me morphine. I kept refusing the anti-nausea drugs, but it finally got to be too much, and I gave in.

A short while after they administered the drug, my hands drew up like a quadriplegic's, my neck went into a spasm and pulled my head over to one side, my face tingled, my legs went into spasms, and my toes splayed out. It was the middle of the night, and I was alone with no roommate. Holy shit! I thought my breathing was going to shut down and I would never take another breath. In the next nanosecond, I remembered that I had a meditation practice and that this might be a good time to use it. I breathed in and out, calming my mind. I thought to myself, *if it is my time to die this is not such a bad way to go. I have had a good life. I have no regrets.* I let go of life and prepared to die. It was a very peaceful and beautiful experience. I kept breathing. I realized after a moment or two that I was not going to die, and frankly was a little disappointed. I was ready.

The nurses came in at some point in response to my pushing the call button and dashed out again. They came back a few minutes later with an injection of muscle relaxant, which counteracted the effects of the anti-nausea drug. I had already been in abject misery before this incident. The leg squeezers kept me awake, the catheter in my bladder was uncomfortable, the IV in my arm was hurting, and the oxygen tube in my nose was irritating. I asked the nurses to remove everything and change my sheets as they were soaked with sweat. They did, and I invited them nicely (well, thinking back, maybe not so nicely) to leave me alone and not disturb me until morning. They agreed, and I went to sleep a changed person.

I no longer fear death. The Buddha tells us that until you give up your fear of death you will not begin to live. He is absolutely correct. Death is a wonderful thing. I sat looking over the brink and it was magnificent. Every religion in the world says we are going to a better place. Why don't people believe it? I am curious now about what happens next in a way I never was before. I am ready to go and find out.

After the surgery, I refused to see the oncologist because I would have refused any treatment they offered me. Cancer is a chronic disease, and ten years between detectable tumors is an acceptable risk to me. It makes no sense to me to kill off my immune system when I need it most. I believe people die from the effects of chemo as often as from cancer itself. I don't see the difference between the ritual of torturing people in the Inquisition and the ritual of administering chemo, for in both if a body survives they are thought to be true believers and they get to live. I am convinced that it is the experience of "suffering" (in a Judeo-Christian culture that values suffering) that cures the patients, not the chemo. I am comfortable living in the "don't know." I have no idea if my cancer has metastasized, and I am not going to worry about it. If something else pops up, I will deal with it in that moment.

Not long after my surgery in 2006, I fell madly in love, head over heels in love like I had not since I was a young woman. It didn't last long and ended without disastrous results. It was clear to me later that it was life itself I had fallen in love with, not a human being. That affair with life continues. There are little deaths each day, a disappointment, an unfulfilled expectation, a lapse in remembering how good I am, but if I remind myself not to fear these little deaths, I go merrily along my way. It frees me up to be present. If you give up the fear of being judged by others along with judging yourself, a silly spontaneous happiness sets in. Think for a moment about what keeps you from talking with strangers on the bus, from calling an estranged relative, or from taking a risk of any sort. It is fear. Fear that the stranger will think you are weird. Fear that your estranged relative will reject you once again. Fear that you will fail or get hurt if you take a risk. It's all smoke and mirrors in your head. The reality is that most strangers are happy to talk to you, and most relatives hope you will call, and the bottom line is that you will never achieve happiness without taking a risk.

The side effect of giving up the fear of dying and all the little deaths is gratitude. Pure, unadulterated, great-full-ness for all that has been provided to me. This is my daily default position. I am so very grateful for all the blessings in my life, even for my disability for taking me on such an interesting journey, and even for my pain calling me to be present every moment. I am grateful for every person who has smiled at me on the street, grateful for my friends who have stuck by me all these years, and grateful for my family for loving me unconditionally since I was born.

I would not be the person I am today without my faith. I am grateful for the Buddha, the Dharma (the teachings) and the Sangha (the community). The Buddha figured out that the key to happiness 2,500 years ago was to let go of the past and future and live in the present, for everything changes every minute (impermanence), and no one thing has inherent value over another (equanimity). I sit at my desk writing this book beneath a poster of eleventh-century wooden Kwan Yin (Guanyin), the bodhisattva of compassion, from China. Her life-sized statue is housed at the Honolulu Academy of Arts, where I have sat at her feet since I was a little girl. Off to the right of my desk is Hotei, the little fat laughing Buddha atop my TV. To the right of that I have an altar with a collection of Guanyin statues on an antique camphorwood trunk. I have tried to make my living space as much like a *zendo* meditation hall as I can. I keep my space free from clutter, I make my bed every day, and I wash the dishes after every meal. Order in my environment encourages peace in my soul.

Chapter 11

My Trip to South America

I n 2007 I received a postcard offering a deal of a lifetime for a three-week cruise across the Atlantic from Lisbon to Buenos Aires. It was a twofer deal, and my friend Stanley stepped up to the plate and volunteered to go along. It was with an English cruise line whose name I have agreed not to mention as part of the agreement to refund my entire ticket. More about this later.

We had to change planes in Frankfort, Germany, on the way. The Jetway was broken, and we had to deplane in the middle of the field. Lufthansa had no accessible ramps for such an event and sent three burly paramedics (two men and one woman) out to carry me off the plane in an aisle chair. They put Stanley and me in a van and drove us to the baggage entrance, where they dropped us off at the disability waiting area. It was a lovely space with accessible bath-rooms, snacks, coffee, and three very helpful young women who checked me in, got me a boarding pass, and escorted me to the plane in time for my flight. It was a curious mix of inaccessibility getting off the plane and everything you could want in the way of accessibility once you were inside the terminal.

Our first night in Lisbon, we went out to dinner at Ribadouro on Avenue da Liberdade near the hotel. It was located on the point of a three-sided building with four wide, treacherous marble steps with no hand rail leading down into the restaurant. Magically, four waiters materialized and carried me down the steps shouting directions to each other the entire time, but luckily no one listened to each other, and we made a safe landing. Once down on the dining floor, the waiters rearranged the entire restaurant so I could roll easily to a table. Quite a production!

The next day we boarded the ship at the cruise ship dock. It was an older vessel built in the seventies. They had made some attempt to make the ship accessible, but it was still difficult to get around. My room, however, was very nice; they had opened up two adjacent rooms to make room for the accessible bathroom. So we had a very large cabin.

The ramps at the outside doorways were very short and steep. Some had automatic doors attached to them, and some didn't. If I was unaccompanied I could not open the doors that were not equipped with automatic openers.

After settling in, we dressed and went to dinner. Every night was a culinary overload of the senses: three appetizers, three soups, two salads, four entrees, and three desserts. You could have as much as you wanted, and if you didn't like it you could have something else. Our waiter was a droll fellow. One night when Duck Leg was on the menu, he asked if I would like the right leg or the left leg without cracking a smile. It took me a minute to figure out it was a joke. Another night I told him I was allergic to tomatoes and he asked if I was also allergic to "tomahtos."

The next day we docked in Madeira, where we went ashore using the gangplank. It was very steep and moved around some. It took three deckhands to bump me down the steps.

Madeira is a beautiful jewel of an island with majestic volcanic cliffs rising up out of the water to sharp green peaks sprinkled with white houses with red tile roofs. Tropical vegetation, vineyards, and bananas grow everywhere. I had asked about an accessible tour, but there was none available, so with considerable effort I boosted myself onto the bus with my arms. Our tour took us down to a little village by the sea, up amazingly steep valleys, across the plateau in the center of the island, and finally to lunch at the far end of the island.

It was quite an ordeal to get me back on to the ship in Madeira. I had to wait quite a while on the dock, and then finally it took three deckhands pushing me up a very steep gangway. It is a very uncomfortable way to travel, three strangers bending in close to you, sweating, straining, and all the time trying not to make me feel bad that

I was a burden, when I was so obviously one. I also never feel quite safe in these situations, as I have no idea what training or experience these men have with the proper handling of wheelchairs. I gave instructions to them, but none of them were native English speakers.

We crossed the equator on the second day out in the Atlantic. Those of us who had not crossed before were assembled on the sun deck for an initiation into Neptune's kingdom. They took me aside and did not let me participate with the other passengers. I was asked to kiss one fish head, and then they rolled me off to the side while the other passengers were also made to kiss the fish and were pelted with gobs of leftover spaghetti and then smeared with blue frosting. And, of course, they had to throw the Captain in the pool. It was all great fun, but I regretted that I never got to be in midst of the goings-on.

One of the evening waiters was quite solicitous of me in the dining room. The first night he pushed my wheelchair up the ramp in the dining room. The second night he pushed it as far as the elevator. The third night he came in the elevator with me; Stanley had an errand to run and left me alone with the waiter. He pushed me off the elevator and down the passageway to my room. I told him I was fine now and thanks for his help, but he insisted. I gave him my room key, and he opened the door. He pushed me into the room, and as he did he ran his hands down the sides of my body. I whirled the wheelchair around, yelling at him to get the fuck out of my room, and he left in a hurry.

I met with the head waiter and told her what he had done. I don't think she believed me entirely, although later the waiter did come to apologize and used the time to tell me all about his wife. His wife was also on the cruise, and she came over and showed me pictures of their children. How did the tables turn here so I was put in a position of having to "forgive" him and to make nice with his wife? Was this discrimination or what? I can just see the head waiter saying to this man that she failed to recognize as a sexual predator that the old lady in the wheelchair was probably confused so go apologize. He was transferred to another section of the dining room, so I never had to deal with him face to face again. He should have been fired. It was a lesson in vulnerability. Before I lived life in a wheelchair, no one had ever done anything like that to me before. But the worm had turned. I was now a vulnerable old woman in a wheelchair. Really made me mad.

Our first stop in Brazil was Salvador. The crew informed me of a new policy at the last minute as we gathered to disembark at the top of the gangplank. It seems that the main office of the cruise line and crew had been in a debate since leaving Lisbon about helping people in wheelchairs on and off the ship. The main office finally ordered the crew to stop helping just before we docked, telling them they would be fired if they assisted me off the ship. I knew nothing of this until they refused to help me off the ship in Salvador. Their brochure said that I needed to bring someone with me to assist me on board, and I had brought Stanley to do that.

But they changed their policy about the gangplank in the middle of my cruise.

Did they think I was just going to sit on the ship for another two weeks and not get off at Rio de Janeiro or Buenos Aires? I had ordered a special accessible tour of Salvador, which was waiting for me at the bottom of the gangplank—a nonrefundable tour. So I assessed the situation carefully, lowered myself out of my wheelchair onto the deck, scooted on the floor over to the gangplank, and with my gloriously well-developed shoulder muscles bumped myself down on my butt to the bottom. The crew and my fellow passengers were horrified. Ha! You TABs (temporarily able-bodied) don't know how to think outside the box! No legs, no help, you use what you got, and I got shoulders. Another passenger brought my wheelchair down, and off I went on my tour of Salvador, Brazil.

A crew member greeted me at the bottom of the gangplank upon my return and asked that I remain in my wheelchair. I did while he and the Officer of Deck communicated with the Captain. There were many phone calls back and forth. After a while, my cabin steward and his friends came by on their way back from liberty and asked if I needed help. I said I did, and they swooped me up the gangplank before anyone had time to tell them not to do it. The Captain and I had a talk that night, and he explained their dilemma. The crew wanted to help, but the main office said no.

The next stop was Rio de Janeiro. We made landfall at noon, and it was like sailing into Disneyland: tall green hills, the giant Jesus on the mountain in the background, Sugarloaf to our left, old forts guarding the city on our right, little islands everywhere. The sun was shining; birds were wheeling and dipping. A flock of geese flew just above the surface of the water in a perfect V. The frigate birds hovered up above. Then the beaches came into view: Ipanema! Copacabana! Then the city tucked under the hills, and a huge, very beautiful bridge came into view. Everyone was at the rail oohing and ahhing. It was love at first sight.

I ordered a private tour of Rio. But we had the same struggle at the gangplank. The Captain finally gave permission to the crew to off-load me. I was delighted to find out that my guide, Marta, was also a Buddhist. We had a great day together. The first stop was the Corcovado and the giant Jesus. The tram station was lively and crowded. I enjoyed being out in the city surrounded by people who live there and hearing Portuguese spoken. The tram arrived, and the attendant moved everyone aside so I could get on. But the little wooden ramp didn't fit in the door. He moved the ramp to another door and found it blocked by a pillar. The attendant hollered to the train driver to move up a bit. He did, and with a little help from fellow passengers we got in. I cannot imagine this happening in the U.S. No one got mad or impatient; everybody as just going with the flow. The rest of the people piled in after us, and at the last moment a samba band, three men with instruments, squeezed into the last remaining inch in the aisle and started playing. Two young women got up and danced. Everyone sang along with the band as we made our way up a very steep mountain. I was in seventh heaven.

At the top there was no elevator to take me the last hundred feet of escalator to the statue. Without missing a beat, an attendant rolled me onto the escalator, and up we went. It was quite a thrill. From the top you can see all of Rio. The statue is on the very top of the highest mountain, and there is a 360-degree view. Folks lay on their backs on the sidewalk trying to get close-up pictures of the statue. At the café my guide insisted that I have a delicious cashew fruit drink. The cashew nut we are familiar with is actually the seed of a large squarish yellow fruit and not a nut at all. The drink we had was made from the meat of the fruit after the seeds were extracted.

The next day, after the usual debate at the gangplank, two fellow passengers and Stanley carried me down to the dock. Our first stop was the Museu do Indio, a magnificent display about the native people of Brazil. The museum, on the second floor, was accessible by a long flight of steps. Four young men appeared out of nowhere and carried me up. The museum was charming: lots of videos, artifacts, music—a very nice exhibit of the native peoples of that area. The men magically reappeared when it came time to leave the museum.

Then we went to the beach—the famous Ipanema Beach. It was packed. The beach itself was very wide. There were no trees but lots of umbrellas and awnings. A very wide, very long sidewalk with a serpentine mosaic pattern in light and dark gray filled with vendors, coffee stands, and snack bars lined the beach. Everywhere I looked were beautiful tanned bodies, men, women, young and old. It was gorgeous in every direction. The beach was surrounded by green hills. There were little islands offshore. The waves were huge and made very deep, round tubes as they crashed into the shore. A good portion of the crowd was on bikes or in-line skates or playing volleyball, or something like volleyball with their feet.

I could not get near the ocean, and it would have been too rough for me to get in if I could have. Our cruise line had a deal with a hotel across from the beach so we could shower and use their pool. I am a very good swimmer, and it had been weeks since I had a chance to swim. The lifeguard came over and assisted me into the pool. I really didn't need help, but he was very cute, so I let him. I took off swimming laps. When I got out he came over and talked with me. I could tell he was quite amazed that an old crippled woman swam like that! Made my day.

Finally, regretfully, it was time to return to the ship and depart for Buenos Aires. And there I was again: begging permission to come aboard. Finally they carried me up the gangplank. The next day we docked at Montevideo, Uruguay, but I was worn out from the battles at the gangplank, so I stayed on board.

We arrived in Buenos Aires the next day. If Rio is an energetic samba girl, Buenos Aires is a dignified older woman with a mantilla in her hair, wearing a dress with a high lace collar. Rio: samba; Buenos Aires: tango! It looked like Paris with beautiful wide boulevards, quaint buildings, and great shopping. We went to see Evita's Pink Palace and the famous balcony where she and her husband used to give speeches, but we didn't cry for her there. We took a tour of the city and wound up at a Tango Show for dinner.

The show was endless! There was one very serious, passionate tango after another, after another, after another, and then an Indian group, and then an Evita impersonator singing, you guessed it, "Don't Cry for Me, Argentina." Then there was more tango and yet another tango and then a gaucho swinging steel balls around on a leash banging them rhythmically on the floor. The evening finally ended with some famous guy who playing the bandonion (a small accordion). I felt like we had been there for days!

We were each served a huge steak that looked like it weighed three pounds. The woman next to me ordered it rare, and I nearly puked at the sight of her stuffing those bloody hunks of raw meat down her throat. I cut off a reasonable portion of my steak and handed the remainder to a very surprised waiter. When the steaks arrived, everyone at the table exclaimed that they could never eat so much meat. But they did, every one of them. I have to admit, it was the best steak I have ever eaten.

The next day I took a bus tour out to a ranch on the pampas. I was getting quite adept at getting on and off the bus by now. It was a lovely place with horses, gauchos, open spaces, birds, and more steak. Lunch was yet another orgy of eating. Not only did those enormous steaks reappear, but now there were sausages, four enormous salads, and endless bottles of wine and beer. Then, of course, the obligatory tango show. Thank God this one was shorter. And better—the couple dancing was older and more sensual. The band started playing songs everyone knew, and folks started dancing in the aisles. There were probably five hundred people there, and only about thirty of us spoke English. We found out that the rest were from all over Latin America. It was a fun party. Reminded me of the old days when we had family luaus in the backyard in Hawaii. Everybody got just a little drunk, had way too much to eat, and danced until they fell down. Everybody had a good time. There were two older women near me clinging fiercely to one another in a dance, twirling about like a dervish. A man tried to cut in, but they tightened their grips and bounced off in a different direction. Good for them!

The next day we disembarked for the last time and stayed in a hotel overnight, and the day after that I caught a plane home. I met a nice young fellow on the plane who had been in the jungle studying the natives and because he had contracted a serious disease was returning to the U.S. for treatment. The flight home took twenty hours.

After I got home I got to thinking about all I had to put up with on that ship, and I wrote a letter to management requesting a refund. I didn't identify myself as a disability advocate. I wanted to see what they would say to an ordinary passenger. Well, to no one's surprise they blew me off. So I wrote another letter.

Let me introduce myself, I said. I was until recently the Associate Director of the Disability Rights Council, where it was my privilege to prepare lawsuits against companies in violation of the Americans with Disabilities Act. I am also an occasional contributor to *New Mobility* magazine, and here is the web link to my latest article, and so on. I was humiliated by having to go down the gangplank on my butt and further humiliated by having to beg at every port to get on and off the ship. I was molested by a waiter, and little was done about it. A full refund for my cruise, including my airfare, arrived with nearly the speed of return mail. Also included was a letter, of course, that disavowed any liability or blame. Geez! What a pain in the ass. In a world where companies are falling all over themselves to become accessible, I guess somebody needs to play the Neanderthal.

Chapter 12

Diminished Capacity

The longer I am disabled, the more I continue to be frustrated by the governmental agencies designed to "serve" us. I have become increasingly aware that these agencies are flawed at their philosophical core. The American government has developed policies that require us to jump through hoop after hoop to demonstrate our "worthiness" to receive the pittance they hand out. These policies increase our stress and actually exacerbate our disabilities. The people working in these agencies have an impossible task of trying to provide much-needed services with their hands tied by the policies. The Social Security Administration routinely turns down applications, making seriously disabled people apply repeatedly before finally approving them. To add fuel to the frustration, the agencies providing food stamps, housing, and vocational rehabilitation all have different eligibility criteria for their services.

It has been a rude awakening that the governmental agencies designed to help people with disabilities for the most part do a piss-poor job of it. Be prepared to become your own best advocate. The systems are horribly complicated, devilishly convoluted, and will make you jump through hoops that are just plain nonsensical. The worst part, however, is that you have to engage this nonsense while you yourself are in a diminished capacity. As I laid there in the rehab hospital I had no fricking idea who to contact, what to apply for, or even what was possible. And there was no one officially to tell me. The hospital social worker met with me for about five minutes, and literally the only information she gave me was the Social Security 800 number. This was awfully reminiscent of when I was first diagnosed with breast cancer in 1995 and I was expected to become an instant expert on what to do while reeling from the thought that I had a deadly disease.

Heretofore (have always wanted to use that word in a sentence!), I never depended on a government agency for anything. I had never been on welfare, unemployment insurance, or Medicaid. I had lived a privileged middle-class life, born into a family that didn't want for a thing, was well educated and earned a good salary. I have observed an unwitting collusion between the policies of the Social Security Administration, the housing agencies, and the food stamp administration to ensure that the disabled remain poor and especially remain out of the workforce.

Many years ago, as part of my Master's in Social Work, I took a course called The History of Welfare. I learned there that our "helping" systems in the U.S. government—welfare, food stamps, disability insurance, and medical insurance—are all based on the Elizabethan notion of the unworthy poor. Poverty and disability were the fault of the individual as he or she had somehow fallen from God's grace. The Old Testament is filled with stories about how God blessed the righteous by making them rich. Based on this ridiculous premise, the United States has developed systems that are needs based instead of focusing on whether people are "worthy" of assistance. The burden of proof falls on the client to prove he or she is needy instead of deserving. The underlying motto of these agencies is "you shall become poor and remain so." The perception that we are unworthy and not valued by society results in policies that diminish our capacity for independence. The reality of their service delivery contradicts the mission of these agencies.

It does not matter how many degrees you have or what you were able to earn before you became disabled. Social Security Disability Insurance will now ensure that you live below the poverty line with all the other lazy bastards (the homeless, the welfare mothers, veterans, and so on) who are also trying to rip off the government. We are all suspect and treated accordingly. If you weren't crazy to start with, being exposed to the chaos of all the issues surrounding having a disability and the frustration of dealing with the dysfunctional agencies could push you right over the edge!

The saving grace for me and thousands of others are the Centers for Independent Living (CIL). There are approximately four hundred of these nonprofit grassroots agencies run by people with disabilities across America. Their mission is to advocate for and assist people with disabilities with anything they need. You can locate the CIL nearest you at http://www.ncil.org. They have information on all the agencies you need to contact, information on how to remodel your house, and counseling to help you make sense of everything that has happened to you. In addition to the CIL, I had a mentor, Esme, and her mother, Judith, guided me through the early days of my disability. I do not know what I would have done without them.

The Social Security Administration rules are so complex that if you call the 800 number three times with a complicated question you are likely to get three different answers. Simple answers they can handle, but anything complicated, they drop the ball. If the employees cannot understand the rules, I don't see how we can be expected to.

They also seem confused about whether they really want you to go back to work or not. They have programs like Ticket to Work in which they claim they are trying to put you back in the workforce, and then on the other hand they have very restrictive policies that act as a serious disincentive. They offer Trial Work Periods with such complicated rules that once I had to appeal for two years and go before an Administrative Law Judge before we could settle their claim that I owed them $47,000. The judge took five minutes before deciding that a mistake was made and set aside the penalty.

Why couldn't some employee have made the same determination and saved me two years of agony? I think it was because I was being punished (unworthy poor that I am) for violating the rules. This from an agency whose mission it is to assist me.

Based on my status with SSA, I am allowed to earn an additional $720 a month. But if I earn $721 a month my *entire* benefit for that month is forfeited. My entire benefit of $1,400 for daring to make one extra dollar, and to add insult to injury, there is always the threat that I will be de-enrolled hanging in the air. Why can't there be an offset like with regular Social Security benefits? If you are an hourly wage earner it is nerve-wracking to always be making sure your hours do not exceed the maximum. I was penalized once because the bookkeeper made a mistake and added a week's worth of work into the next month.

The SSA prorates your benefits on your previous earnings, so why can't they prorate your earnings after you are disabled? They could design a rate chart that links earnings to benefits that would allow us to earn a percentage of what we used to earn. Why should I have to live below the poverty line just because I am disabled? Why? Because the unwritten rule of the unworthy poor is that if you receive government benefits you will live in poverty. I can't wait until I am sixty-six years old and get out from under SSDI restrictions. At sixty-six I will switch over to regular Social Security and then live under those restrictions and tax liabilities. God willing, I will still be able to work then.

To make things more complicated, I live in government-subsidized housing, where my rent is calculated based on one third of my income. So if I earn $720 a month, $200 is taken out for taxes, my rent is increased by $240, and I get home with $280 for forty hours of work. It hardly seems worth it. I earned more in 1965 as a student in the college library. It strikes a blow to my middle-class, well-educated pride. It is a lesson in humility I could live without. These policies discourage people with disabilities from working when ironically not working and not contributing is part of the stigma placed on us. It's a Catch 22 dilemma: the agencies designed to assist actually work against us by creating an impossible bureaucracy through which no one can easily maneuver.

I applied for food stamps because my minimum monthly expenses were exceeding my income. After I filled out a ten-page application, providing information about every private part of my life, they turned me down. It seems my SSDI payment exceeded the income limits for food stamps by a goddamned fifteen dollars. So I am poor enough not to be able to meet my monthly expenses but not poor enough to receive full assistance. Does this strike anyone else as ridiculous?

I had to fill out a similar application to apply for senior housing and provide access to the same invasion of privacy as for the food stamps application. But luckily for me, the housing income requirements are different. One could ask why all the agencies have different eligibility requirements, but I won't go there….

In addition to the insults heaped upon us from SSA, food stamps, and the housing authority, the IRS is not much better. Why do they tax the poor? I get so little money as it is, so why do they force me to stretch my dollars even further each month? I get the money back at tax time, so why not let me have it during the year and call it even in April? Surely they could calculate a different tax rate that will even out and not take money out of the mouths of the poor without me having to lie about having ten dependents. I am most willing to contribute to FICA and unemployment insurance (for which I am pretty sure I am not eligible), but please leave me the rest.

Finally, I have to say that the people working at these agencies were for the most part very nice to me. They weren't always informed, didn't always know the answers, but mostly treated me kindly. My complaint is about the policies, not the individuals working there. I realize that even though I am biracial, I look and sound white and enjoy all the privileges granted to white people in America. But I know that others of racial or ethnic minorities do not always have the same experience with these agencies. They have to navigate through the same irrational systems while at the same time have to deal with the racism that is rampant in the USA.

Chapter 13

Discrimination

"*At the root of discrimination is the idea of selection and personal preference. We choose some people as friends and stay away from others because they have drug habits, use offensive language in referring to certain people, steal from us, or pose a threat. Being discriminating is not a bad thing but the problem comes when institutions and groups use the power of their dominant positions to 'stay away' or 'push away' or 'deny access' or 'deny rights' to whole groups of people, assigning stigma/ threat to all, penalizing groups/members for differences from the dominant powerful that do not, in fact, pose a threat to others.*" Melva Ware

As I continue to live with my disability, it has become clearer to me how much my environment affects my experience. I first learned this lesson in Italy, where an unwelcoming environment devastated my self-esteem. No ramps, curb cuts, or accessible buses stated loud and clear that I was not welcome, as clearly as the "Whites Only" drinking fountain signs a generation ago made it clear who was welcome and who was not. Eighteen-inch curbs, stairs everywhere, and crowded restaurants with no room for my wheelchair made me feel unwelcome and oh so very crippled. But on the other hand, back in the United States, wide aisles, buses with lifts, and accessible bathrooms made me feel welcome, independent, and powerful.

As an old, biracial, lesbian Buddhist in a wheelchair, I bump up against some form of discrimination on a daily basis. If it's not an inaccessible restaurant, then it's a joke about gays, or someone choosing to hire a younger person, or someone wishing me a Merry Christmas even though they know I am a Buddhist. I am reminded moment to moment that I am not in the mainstream, and the world, for the most part, chooses to draw a circle with me on the outside.

Partly because I was raised in multicultural Hawaii and partly because I was a child of the sixties, I have spent my life working for civil rights. As a student at the University of Hawaii in the early sixties, I raised money to send two other students to the voter registration drive in Mississippi. Martin Luther King, Jr., James Farmer, and a Black Panther representative (whose name I have forgotten) came and spoke to us in 1964. It made quite an impression.

In the early seventies I was working for the Girl Scouts in Tampa, Florida, where I became involved in two causes. The first was the burgeoning women's movement and the other the integration of the summer camps. My boss at the Girl Scouts, Mildred Whigery, was very interested in what was going on with the women's movement and sent me as her representative to a variety of events. It was mind-boggling. As a teenager I had railed against my mother for being a doormat. I so wanted her to be strong and tell my father to go to hell. But she was child of the twenties and could not see her way clearly to do so, and she attempted suicide twice instead while I was in high school. In 1970 read Betty Friedan's *The Feminine Mystique*. It finally explained to me the whole contradiction between who women really are and how society devalues them. No wonder my mother tried to kill herself; she was unable to resolve the contradiction.

I was at the time involved in a relationship with a woman who had very definite ideas about gender roles: she was the butch (male role), and I was the femme (female role). But my infant feminist self started to question why I was doing all the things a wife would do when I was a woman living with a woman. The day the new lawnmower arrived and I assembled it was the beginning of the end of our relationship. I had stepped out of my role, and I was headed out the door.

As a Girl Scout executive I was part of a team of community leaders called in to assist the local high school counselor after a race riot erupted there. Talk about jumping into the fire—it was like Race Relations 101. I had only my instincts to go on. I was very naïve about how the race thing played out in the South, or anywhere else for that matter. I offered my camps for a retreat and in that way got to participate with the students, faculty, and people from other community agencies in a weekend retreat. The students asked that the bus drivers be included as they spent many hours a day on the buses and the drivers were working-class white Southerners and a little behind the integration curve. I wasn't so naïve when the weekend came to a close.

Later that same year the American Camping Association (ACA) issued an edict to Florida's camps to integrate them within one year or lose their ACA accreditation. I received a grant from them to train black camp counselors in preparation for the next summer season. I learned a lot from those young people about white assumptions. White folks thought going out in the woods, living in a shack with a canvas roof, and using a pit latrine was fun, a nice change from how they usually lived. The black counselors thought it was like rolling back the clock and going to visit their grandparents. They were barely one generation away from when some black people in the South lived like that. White folks thought it was fun to wear camping clothes and get dirty. The black counselors wanted to dress nicely and were not keen on sitting in the dirt around a campfire. I quickly understood that the two issues of race and women's rights were not unrelated. I was at the time still thinking I was white and had not claimed my biracial status. There was, however, a small voice speaking to me deep inside saying I really didn't think like the other white people I knew.

In the eighties I was embroiled up to my eyebrows with women's rights, working in Washington, DC, for a number of women's organizations. I worked first for the National Women's Health Network (NWHN) on a project involving Depo-Provera. The FDA was about to approve it as an injectable contraceptive, and we opposed it. The drug was quite clearly proved to cause cancer. I got quite an education into the politics of women's health, reproductive health, and international women's health. Upjohn, the manufacturer of Depo-Provera, was promoting the drug in Africa. We prevailed, and I learned an important lesson about just how loud a mouse can roar. We were a small organization of nine thousand women who took on the big guns and won! The FDA did not approve the drug for use as an injectable contraceptive at that time. Of course, Upjohn continued to apply, and the drug was eventually approved.

The race issue kept coming up for me. Belita Cowan and Billy Avery founded the Black Women's Health Network while I was working at the NWHN. I observed Belita's very skillful organizing techniques. She stayed very much in the background and coached Billy, a wonderful black woman, on how to raise money and get the BWHN organized. Belita was white and didn't think it politically correct for a white woman to lead a black organization. It was the best example of a win-win situation I had ever seen.

Then in 1983 I met Melva Ware while working at the League of Women Voters. Melva's insight and articulation about race in America contributed profoundly to my understanding of what was going on. She was the first black person who opened up to me and let me see what life was like for her. She will tell you, though, that it was me who opened up to her and that I was the only white person she knew who got it.

In the eighties I also became involved with the Gay Women's Alternative. We met weekly with a program of interest to lesbians. We offered a variety of programs on arts, literature, music, psychology, and politics. It was the beginning of my education on gay rights. I marched in the marches, attended protests, and read a lot of books. We sponsored an annual conference on aging as a lesbian called Passages. Our elders would speak at these conferences telling us what it was like in the days when lesbians were regularly beaten up, fired, or sometimes even killed if it became known what they were. I hardly drew a breath in those days that was not related to the civil rights of someone.

In 1983 I was working for the League of Women Voters and was sent to Raleigh, North Carolina, to meet with a chapter there. They asked me how to integrate their chapter. I said it really is not hard; just invite your black neighbors and friends to join. There was dead silence. But it led into a productive discussion of how integration is not as easy as one would think. From 1990 to 1995 I was in charge of organizing chapters nationwide for the Older Women's League (OWL). I traveled the country meeting with groups of older women and received a crash course on age discrimination.

It was a good primer, as I now struggle on a daily basis with the same issues of health, housing, and income that those women spoke about. I was greatly inspired by the women I met through OWL—sassy old women and wonderful role models.

In January 1995, shortly after Newt Gingrich's mother called Hillary Clinton a bitch on national television, I was to give a presentation on organizing to the Business and Professional Women's annual meeting in DC. I was forty-nine years old and the Field Service Director of the Older Women's League. The presenter preceding me, a man from AARP, had shared with the women ten really, really boring rules of organizing. After his presentation I stood up, took the microphone, and in my bright red suit with high-necked white blouse, marched down into the audience. I reminded them about Mrs. Gingrich's remark, paused, and then said quite dramatically, "I don't know about you, but I am ASPIRING to be A BITCH!" The audience, mostly older women, hooted and hollered in agreement. "Not only do I want to be a bitch, I want to be an old bitch!" They cracked up and laughed for minutes. I think now I may have finally accomplished my goal.

In the late nineties, after decades of civil rights work on behalf of people of color, women, the elderly, and the LBGT community, I joined the ranks of the disability advocates. It seems only natural to bring my arsenal of organizing techniques to my newly found cause.

Early in my disabled life I attended a rally at the Supreme Court about MiCASSA (Medicaid Attendant Community Services and Supports Act), which is a law allowing individuals to use money currently earmarked for nursing homes to be used instead to care for themselves in their own homes. The crowd was a mixed bag of folks, with every disability represented. The organizers packed us tightly in at the bottom of the steps to the Supreme Court, about twenty people deep. I was sitting right next to a young man who had no arms or legs. We had been out all day at rallies, and his urine collection bag needed changing. It smelled. On my other side was a young woman with severe cerebral palsy. She could not talk and drooled constantly. She also smelled. I sat there for a brief moment wondering what in the hell I was doing surrounded by these people. This was not me, the chatter in my head was keen to point out, and I was a healthy, high-functioning paraplegic. I took a breath and looked around. The truth was I had everything in common with the people gathered there. A great shift in my identity was taking place, yet another bleeping opportunity for growth. I took another breath and started a conversation with the man next to me.

Where does this seemingly natural aversion to people with disabilities start? One can imagine that back in the time when we descended from trees and went into the caves that a disabled member of the clan was a liability. Infants with birth defects were probably killed because no one could care for them. A disabled adult could no longer participate in either the hunting or the gathering of food. It seems possible to me that "value to the clan" could be the ancient source of prejudice against people with disabilities. But I suspect there is more to it than that. We all ask ourselves the existential questions: "Who am I?" and "Am I doing the right thing?" I know who I am by comparing myself to others. I am taller or shorter, thinner or fatter, lighter skinned or darker skinned, can run swiftly or walk with a limp. All these things define us. Societies provide the answer to the "Are we doing the right thing?" question. Every society sets up rules, laws, and customs to define who we are as a people. In order to define ourselves as an ethnicity or culture, we need to limit the definition of who we are, and somebody will be shuffled to the outskirts to establish the border.

In 1995 at the UN Fourth World Conference on Women in Beijing, China, I attended a workshop about the rise of fundamentalism in all the world's religions. The panel leading the discussion consisted of women theologians from around the world representing every major religion. In their discussion of the rise of rigid fundamentalism in each of their religions, they were quick to point out that it has been accompanied with a rise in prejudice and discrimination. The theologians concluded that people want certainty, they want to know the rules, and they want to know what is right and what is wrong. In this age of world media where even the poorest farmer in India has access to CNN on television, the differences we once thought separated "them" from "us" are now beginning to blur. There was a time when geographical, ethnic, and race differences were clear, but now all the young men worldwide dress like American rap stars, and everyone drinks Coca-Cola and wears Levi's. The fundamentalist responding to the need to know who we are claims that their true religion will reestablish the boundaries and provide comfort in reestablishing the borders. This is who "we" are, they say. But unfortunately these borders encourage prejudice and discrimination and usually violence. In an age of indeterminate genders, multiculturalism, hyphenated ethnicity, and ADA access for all, some people feel the need to draw the line somewhere to know who they are.

In the past eleven years I have experienced every barrier in the disability world. I frequently run into physical barriers like inaccessible curbs, restaurants, bathrooms with a handicap sign on the door and no accessible stalls inside, or perhaps all the spare chairs in the restaurant are piled in the bathroom hallway. I have bumped up against just plain silly attitudes, a restaurant hostess talking only to my companion and not to me, or I call a restaurant and ask if they are accessible and they say yes, well, except for the two steps at the entrance, or no disabled people ever come here, so we didn't think we needed to build a ramp, or this is a historic site so we don't need to build a ramp. I went to the urologist at Kaiser in DC, and there was no accessible examination table with adjustable heights. Excuse me? Who are the patients of an urologist? Old people and disabled people. Auurrrgh!

I also get left on the sidelines a lot. I can't really call it discrimination; it is more just a reality of life. I am in a wheelchair, and I am not rolling over the sand to a ceremony on the beach. It's not my friends' faults that they were all living in inaccessible housing before I became disabled and now I cannot visit them in their homes. I only know of one person, Linda Royster, director of the Disability Rights Council, who went to extremes to make her house accessible, but then she was dedicated to the community. I went to a birthday party recently and spent the whole time on the lanai in the front yard because I could not get into the house; someone had to bring me a plate of food. Give the hostess credit though; she made everyone come outside to give the blessing. It was a double-edged sword. I was glad to be included but felt a little bad that I was a bother to everyone. My ego is intact, but sometimes always having to make people accommodate me gets to me on occasion. I know it's my right, and I know most people are happy to do it, but I guess it falls in the "I wish the world were different" category. I wish they didn't have to do it.

So, what do I know about discrimination from being an old, biracial, lesbian Buddhist in a wheelchair? Discrimination is more about ignorance than evil intent; it's more about allowing yourself to be blind to what is right under your nose than setting out to deliberately exclude someone. It's more about cutting a corner to save a few dollars in construction than a malicious plan to make sure a person in a wheelchair is left downstairs when the party is up on the deck. So, I say, WAKE UP! Don't leave it all to us in the wheelchairs to point out the obvious.

Chapter 14

The Social Security Administration

I have a love-hate relationship with the Social Security Administration. On one hand I had a wonderful professional experience serving an internship under Susan Daniels, Deputy Commissioner for Disability and Income Security Programs, and on the other hand there have been moments when I could have happily gone postal and blown away the Western Region Office. As I explained in the Diminished Capacity chapter, there are some flaws in the Social Security philosophy, but the bottom line is that I am actually grateful the system exists. Without it I would be begging on the street.

Let's start with the good news. In 2000 I was a PhD candidate at George Washington University in Rehabilitation Counseling. I was required to serve an internship and I was offered a position by Susan. She is a delightful woman in a wheelchair and a great inspiration for me. She also was quite a character. She considered her hair color an accessory, so you never knew what shade of red she would turn up in. She also acquired a King Charles spaniel as a service dog, a cute, cuddly little thing that I suspect was more pet than service animal. But she gathered around her a remarkable collection of women on wheels, and I felt quite privileged to be included among them.

The Ticket to Work program was on the verge of being launched, and the Administration was keen to bring the state Vocational Rehabilitation workers up to speed, especially the Native Americans. The Native Americans have a separate system from the state run Voc Rehab offices. Because of my Native American background, Susan asked me to assist with planning a series of meetings out west for the tribal Voc Rehab workers. We held such a meeting at the Avi Resort and Casino, hosted by the Fort Mojave Indian Tribe, on the California-Nevada border. In a very generous gesture, the Casino provided rooms for all of us and fed us until we were stuffed at every meal. Tribal Voc Rehab workers from all over the Southwest attended. It was my first real contact with Native Americans outside of my father. I was raised in Hawaii by a father who did not like being a half-breed (his term), and he had no contact with other Native Americans. But I loved it; there was something eerily familiar about the people I met. Perhaps my DNA was speaking to me; I don't know.

I told the story of my Native American grandmother lying about her tribal affiliation, claiming to be Hopi when she was really probably Apache. For the first time I had an audience that understood and thought it hilarious.

A few months later we organized a meeting in Fort Collins, Colorado, that was equally interesting to me. I came away with a much clearer understanding of the challenges faced by disabled Native Americans. It ain't a pretty picture. Few jobs are available anywhere near or on the reservations, and the disabled are at the bottom of the list. Some of the tribes still cling to the idea that the person, or the mother, in cases of birth defects, was responsible for causing the disability. There is a small ring of truth to it, as there is a very high rate of so-called crack babies and babies born with fetal alcohol syndrome to Native Americans. The Ticket to Work looked like it was a great idea for the many self-employed artists and crafts persons I met. The program had the possibility of providing much needed capital to get a craft business off the ground.

The Bad News… Before I plunge into all the SSA has done to make my life miserable, just let me say that for the most part they provide much-needed money to us disabled persons, and they do it, once you are determined eligible, with great regularity… as long as you do not deviate one slight whisker from the many, many, many rules. They are the quintessential bureaucracy; the IRS comes in at close second. There are lots of rules that the SSA employee attempting to answer your question over the phone may or may not be aware of. Mostly it works, but when it doesn't, look out!

SSA has a five-month waiting period to declare you eligible for disability insurance. The problem is, of course, from the first moment you are disabled, your income disappears. Conventional financial planning suggests that you keep three months' expenses in a savings account. Even if I had done that, I would still be without income for two months. Before I was disabled, I had just spent my savings building up my massage business and had approximately one month's expenses in my account.

But I made it through the waiting period, as they say, through the kindness of strangers. My friend Brigitte Savage, with whom I had worked at OWL, sent a letter to all the OWL chapters telling them of my plight and to send money. Eighteen months earlier, Deborah Briceland Betts, the new Executive Director who had been on the job one month, fired me, at 4:45 p.m. on a Tuesday afternoon for, as she said, "no reason." I had been there five years, and in that time I had quite successfully doubled the number of chapters from thirty-five to seventy. This was THE most ridiculous thing that ever happened to me. What the hell was she thinking? That she was some big corporate executive giving me fifteen minutes to clean out my office? I had known her for years and thought her a friend. She could have just asked me to leave nicely, and I would have gone (well, with a little severance pay). The women in the chapters were also outraged, but all appeals to the Board fell on deaf ears. But now the women in the chapters had a chance to express their gratitude for my tenure at OWL and donated approximately $13,000, mostly in $25 increments. It was harder, in a way, to get my head around their generosity than it was to be crippled. The money carried me over securely until Social Security Disability Insurance finally kicked in.

Once I started receiving SSDI, I understood that I was entitled to attempt a trial work period in which I could earn a regular salary for nine months. At the end of that time I could continue to work full time and receive no SSDI payments, or I could continue to receive SSDI payments and be restricted to earning $500 a month. If I chose to remain on SSDI and ever exceeded the then $500 restriction even by one dollar, I would forfeit my entire monthly benefit of $1,100. I opted for the trial work period but found that I could not sustain full-time work. The pain in my legs was too extreme, and I didn't have enough energy to work all day.

I attempted a second trial work period three years later, mistakenly thinking that I was eligible three years from the onset of my disability, but it turned out to be three years from the time I was reinstated after the last trial work period, so my calculation was off by almost a year. I found once again after a couple of months that I was not able to sustain full-time work and went back to part-time work.

Three years after I attempted the second trial work period, the fun began. I got notice from the SSA office that I owed $49,556 and was declared ineligible three years retroactively. Yikes! It was payable immediately. The letter said to send a check by return mail. Imagine now that the SSDI check is your sole means of support, you are barely making it month to month, and you get a bill for that amount payable immediately!

Luckily there was an offer of an appeal. I called Susan Daniels, who told me to appeal, and appeal until I had a hearing before the Administrative Law Judge. So I did. It took two years. They sent the same letter about every six months, and I appealed every one. After a few months they sent a letter that said, to quote them exactly, "You are no longer disabled." Well, hallelujah! I will just get right up out of this wheelchair and dance across the floor! The gob'ment has declared me cured! What a bizarre way to word the letter! What they meant was that according to their rules I was no longer eligible. So here we go again. I had to file again. I attempted to file an expedited application. It took six months for the so-called expedited application to be processed, and yet it only takes five month for a regular application. You figure it out; maybe "expedited" means something else there. After many trips to the SSA office and filling out forms each time, I was temporarily reinstated.

I kept appealing the $49,556 bill until finally, two years later, I was allowed a hearing before an Administrative Law Judge. I explained that I had misunderstood the rules. I told him that I had offered this explanation to everyone in the SSA, but no one had listened. In less than five minutes, he banged the gavel and threw my case out. I didn't have to pay anything and was reinstated as a permanent SSDI recipient. For several years after his finding, every letter I got from the SSA said I owed $29,300. I don't know where they got that figure. I submitted a copy of his finding three times to the Western Regional Office before those letters ceased.

But it gets better. About six months after the judge's ruling, I went to the ATM machine to draw out a little money. The receipt said my checking account balance was $14,000. Holy shit! I never had more than a couple hundred dollars in my account. Did the bank make a mistake and put someone else's money in my account? No, it turns out that the SSA had deposited $13,300 directly into my account. I called SSA to find out what had happened.

According to the man I talked to, it wasn't a mistake. I was owed these back payments for when I was declared no longer disabled and reapplied for benefits. I told him that I had never missed a payment, but he insisted I was owed the money. I called a friend who works in the local SSA office and asked what I should do. She said to put it in an interest-bearing account and wait to hear from the SSA. Two months later I got a bill for $8,300, payable immediately. I sent them a check. I waited two years to see if they were going to ask for the rest. They didn't, so I used the money to go to South America on a cruise!

But wait, there's more. After several years of not hearing a word from Social Security except for my check each month, I was once again at the ATM. This time my receipt said I had $19,803 in my account. So I went home, and sure enough it was a direct deposit from the SSA. I live close to the office here in Honolulu and went down there to find out what was going on. The man behind the window asked if I had received a letter. I had not. He said it seemed that a mistake was made seven and a half years ago, and they had failed to give me a $136 raise in my benefit. Seven and a half years ago was when they were de-enrolling me one day and enrolling me the next, and it added up to $19,184. I asked the man behind the window if this was really true or was I going to get a bill shortly asking for it all back. It's true, he said. He stood up and started dancing and singing, "We're in the money, we're in the money!" I could barely believe it. As I rolled out of the office I fell into step with a security guard. He asked me how my day was going. I said they just gave me $19,000. "Wow!" he said. "Vegas, here we come!" I am grateful they saved the money for me, as I would never have done it on my own.

After living for so many years in poverty, after not being able to purchase anything beyond the bare minimum, this was a literal godsend. I cried. I sat in my little apartment and cried. I got goose bumps every time I stopped to think about it. What do you do with such a windfall?

Over the years I had accumulated a sizable credit card debt, almost the same amount as the windfall. A financial planner friend said to invest it. A debt counselor friend said to pay off the credit card. My inner child said let's spend it! Life is uncertain, eat dessert first. So I did all three, sort of. I gave myself permission to spend some. I paid off half the credit card, so I now have some credit if something happens. And I put the rest in an interest-bearing account and made a deal with myself to be conservative about spending, as I will need it to supplement my monthly income for years to come.

The one thing I did spend the money on was to publish this book.

Chapter 15

Vocational Rehabilitation

My first encounter with Vocation Rehabilitation Services in DC 1997 left me unsure about their ability to help. At the time I had no idea how severely disabled I was. I thought I was doing fine, so I asked a friend to push me into the office like I was a helpless cripple so the counselor would think I could do nothing for myself. My counselor led us into the conference room, and we started filling out paperwork. Suddenly, the door was violently thrown open, and a fat, red-faced man burst in, yelling at my counselor to get out because he had use of the room. Well, that made an impression, I can tell you! This place clearly had no respect for human beings! We left the conference room with my counselor shrugging her shoulders by way of an apology. I am happy to report that the man retired shortly after that, but what an introduction.

I had been coached by Judith and Esme to be clear about what I wanted. I requested hand controls for my car and a wheelchair. But you have to understand that I knew nothing about wheelchairs and had no idea what I needed. The salesperson at the wheelchair store was new and mismeasured me (wheelchairs are customized for your height and weight, leg length, and so on). I wound up with a wheelchair that was useless to me, and it spent the next two years in the back of the closet. I was totally ignorant of what was available, and I was at the mercy of an inexperienced salesclerk. I found out later that this happens a lot to persons with disabilities. We are such a small population that some salesclerks don't have much experience dealing with us. Luckily a friend gave me her old chair, and another friend gave me her mother's electric scooter. I eventually purchased a scooter on my own, never thinking for some reason that Voc Rehab would purchase me one.

Two years later in 1999, at my request, I went back to school to get my EdS in Rehab Counseling. The Department of Education was keen to upgrade the education of all the rehab counselors in the U.S. and offered grants to anyone who was already working in the field or who wanted to go into the field. Luckily for me, George Washington University was one of the sites that had grants available.

I already had a Master's in Social Work, so getting a Master's in Counseling seemed like a waste. The administration at the university offered me an opportunity to enter the doctoral program. But as I got into it, I found that I was not interested in doing research; I was a clinician. They then offered me an Education Specialist degree. I would take the same coursework as the doctoral candidates, but I would not have to do a dissertation. Sounded like a good plan to me.

I loved being in school. I was older than the students and most of the faculty. I had years of Re-evaluation Counseling training, and the courses were a breeze. It was like getting a degree for something you already knew how to do. My classmates were always amazed when they saw the tapes of my sessions and asked me lots of questions about how I got the client to cry. Crying, or discharge, as we call it in RC, is our primary methodology; we consider it absolutely necessary to make any progress.

I was to complete an internship for two of my classes. The first was with the Social Security Administration, and the second was at the Voc Rehab office where I was a client. Since I was a graduate student in counseling, at Voc Rehab I was assigned to work with several of the more difficult cases. The plan worked quite well, as the clients really only wanted some attention, and I was available to give it to them. I got to know the other counselors there, and I have to admit that the more I worked with them the more they rose in my esteem. Most of them cared deeply about their clients and tried very hard within a broken-down system to provide services. I have a lot of respect for them now.

I did not need their services until I returned home to Hawaii. My scooter had worn out, and the local office provided me another one since I was still in the workforce. They also provided a sidewalk from the street to my back door and widened my bathroom door so I could get my wheelchair in.

I found out later that was I the poster child for this service. I had clear needs, and I was going to return to the workforce. My advice for anyone needing their services is to be clear about what you need to return to work. Their mission is to support us in any way they can to get us back into the workforce. So it is important to know that they are neither a welfare agency nor a supplier of equipment for people who don't intend to work. But it is up to you to determine what is needed.

Chapter 16

Spirituality

S o why, you ask, am I not overwhelmed? Why do I continue to see the cup as filling up and spilling over in spite of everything? The answer is both simple and complicated. A complicated intersection of time and experiences shaped my spirit and me into a spiritually mature, very happy old lesbian Buddhist in a wheelchair.

I once heard a talk by the Dalai Lama in Washington, DC, on attaining peace in the world. He started out saying, "If you want peace in the world, start by being nice to the person next to you." Then he paused, and we leaned forward, eager for the rest of the message. "That's it," he said. "It's that simple: Just be nice to the person next to you." I do my best to carry that out every day. I smile at strangers. I talk with anyone in my space. I make an effort to include everyone.

Think about it for a moment. What if every person on Earth was nice to the person next to him or her all the time? What if you slowed down and waved to let another car cut in front of you instead of speeding up? What if you smiled and said something nice to a grouchy salesclerk? What if you smiled at the funky, smelly, homeless person instead of looking away disgustedly? What if you gave a harried mom in the grocery store with a screaming two-year-old a hand instead of giving her what we call in Hawaii the stink-eye? What if you gathered up all your courage and talked to your grouchy old neighbor who is probably just lonely and isolated? What a wonderful world this would be.

My Native American/Zen father greatly influenced my early spiritual development. He was raised by a mother who rejected her Native American background and embraced the Spiritualism movement of the twenties. The plot thickens…his mother told him they were Hopi, one of the most deeply spiritual Native American tribes. But it turns out that we are probably Apache. He, however, rejected being a half-breed Indian (which he called himself) and like his mother sought answers elsewhere. All through my childhood he gave dharma talks at the dinner table about the nature of Buddhism, echoes of which I hear now from my Buddhist teachers.

When I was child my father owned a sixteen-foot flat-bottomed skiff called the Kilohana. It resembled a Japanese fishing boat called a sampan, so he painted it sampan blue with darker blue trim and a red interior. We spent many a day out in the boat on the reef about a mile offshore from Lanikai Beach. During low tide the reef rose a foot or so above the water, and you could walk across it from coral head to coral head. It was magical out there. I walked on the coral heads surrounded by a thousand shades of blue water with surf breaking on the outside edge of the reef adding a brilliant white contrast to the blue. Between the coral heads you could see down to the sand bottom of the reef. Hundreds of brightly colored reef fish were visible from the surface. I would let myself down into the spaces between the coral heads into a beautiful surreal world of shadow and color and shapes unknown on the surface. I remember clearly the feeling of the water on my skin and the coolness of it after being heated by the sun. It was effervescent somehow, thrilling and a little scary.

Under the water I would hear little crackling sounds from the tiny shrimp in the sand below. With my face mask I saw enormous schools of *manini* (convict tang) as they swooped over the coral heads like a river, turning this way and that, driven by some unknown engineer, hundreds of little yellowish fish with black stripes flowing back and forth. I also saw large *uhu* (parrot fish) mimic the thousand shades of ocean blue and add to it red and purple as they swam by. Down on the sand bottom red *moana* and ghost-white *weke* fed on small creatures. Hole hole (red squirrel fish) abounded in dark crevices under the coral heads. Once I saw three cuttlefish floating near the outside of the reef; the colors and patterns on their skin changed every few seconds. I nearly drowned because I did not want to go to the surface and take a breath in fear that they would take off.

The reef was not far from the Twin Islands (Mokolua Islands). We would put ashore on the double-humped one to cook our catch. My father built a fire out of driftwood, and my mother cooked the manini on a hibachi. They were small fish barely a half-inch deep, and it only took thirty seconds on a side to cook them. I can taste them to this day. Hot, crispy, smoky, and oh so delicious. You bit down to the bone and pulled the flesh off with your teeth. They tasted like the *limu* (seaweed) they fed on in the reef. We gathered salt off the rocks on the shore as the only spice. We also cooked *kala* (unicorn fish) on the grill. The *kala* has a very thick skin that allows the meat to steam inside of it.

An additional treat was collecting and eating *ophi* (limpet). These little volcano-shaped shells covered every rock along the shore in those days. We ate them raw right out of shell, accompanied with a seaweed that grew next to them. My mother brought *musubi* to accompany these feasts, a rice ball with an Ume plum in the middle, wrapped in nori seaweed. After lunch I lay in the warm sand, looking toward beautiful Lanikai and the hills, listening to the murmur of the nesting birds, feeling as happy as a person could be in this world.

My fondest memory of the boat, though, is one night we were out by the reef. I sat there mesmerized as the moon, big as all outdoors, rose slowly up right between the two islands. I remember the reflection on the water broken up by small waves and ripples around the reef. It was a calm night, and somehow the moonlight made it quiet. All this was laying a groundwork for my burgeoning spiritual self. Times change; places change; we grow up and move on. I am grateful for those magical moments on the reef that have stuck with me all my life.

In my early teenage years my father gave me important lessons on how to focus my chi (life force) using archery, karate, and surfing. He would have me stand very still, pull the bowstring to my chin, and hold it until I felt the universe settle down and my chi was focused. Only then could I release the arrow. Needless to say, I became a very good archer. About the same time he sent me to karate school run by an old Japanese man. The sensei (teacher) taught us to meditate and practice a very disciplined routine of punches and kicks. He whacked me with a stick if I seemed unfocused. Both experiences enhanced my self-confidence and gave me important information about chi that would serve me well later in life.

My father also taught me to body surf. I would hang on to his broad shoulders while he surfed. Not only was it a lesson in focusing your chi, but I also learned how fast to swim to catch a wave that was about to break and when to bail out if it was too dangerous. He often talked about how the ocean teaches you to be honest with yourself. He believed that if you lied to yourself about your abilities regarding the ocean, it would smack you down. He pointed out how the ocean did not care about you; you could talk a good story on land, but in the ocean, if you did not have internal integrity you would be in danger in the water. These were powerful lessons at an early age.

My godfather, Al "Sparky" Putzker, was a squirrely old bachelor who lived on a boat, the Laga, in the Ala Wai Yacht Harbor. He was a small, wiry man smelling of tobacco. He had very stringy muscles, a bald head, and thick glasses. I remember him wearing only shorts and no shirt. He had a few gray hairs on his chest and was very tan. He physically resembled Gandhi in a way. He worked for Raytheon in some sort of technical position.

Sparky raced the Laga every chance he got. His favorite was the overnight race to Pokai Bay. We would sail all day north up the west coast of Oahu, past Honolulu and Barber's Point and finally into the little marina at Pokai Bay. The sail along the coast was breathtakingly beautiful: the blue Pacific, bright white surf along the shore, the green Ko'olau mountains topped with clouds, gorgeous valleys and bays along the way. The ocean breeze was in your face, dolphins surfaced occasionally, and a flying fish or two skittering away from the boat. The green mountains turned to brown the farther north we got toward Waianae. My job was to keep his glasses washed off and his cup filled with cheap red wine and assist with changing the sails.

Once when we broke a shroud off Barber's Point, he and my father sent me up the mast in a boson's chair (a small plank affixed to the main halyard) while the boat swung from side to side with the head of the mast way out over the water. I replaced the broken shroud with a new one and managed to get back to the deck safely. I wasn't too scared, and I was quite proud that they trusted me to do the job. I trusted my father when he said I would be safe. It reinforced a special bond between us.

I am grateful to that geeky old guy for providing me with magical experiences that have stayed with me all my life. As a teenager I was treated as a competent member of the crew, an important lessons for a young person. I rarely get out on the water anymore, but when I do it's not hard to slip right back into the memories of those adventures of my youth.

When I was in high school a missionary family from a Pentecostal church in Texas moved into our neighborhood. One day the mother of the family asked me to read the New Testament. I agreed as I had never been to church nor had any religious instruction other than what my father had said at the dinner table, and I was curious. She hoped, as some Christians do, that I would find Christ and be reborn just by reading the Gospel. I read the whole thing and found it an interesting story, but I have to admit that the reborn thing slipped right by. I talked with her after I finished reading it, and she remarked that she had never met a heathen who was so moral. Heathen? Was it only Jesus Christ who created moral human beings? I had many Buddhist friends who lived ethical lives. I believe my thoughts were a big eye-opener for her, not to mention a reassurance for me that there was more than one way to heaven.

In college I spent a great deal of time with an old family friend, Kay Cromwell, a devout Christian Scientist. She lived a deeply spiritual life and was a great role model for me for years. She took me to a number of Wednesday night meetings at which people told remarkable stories about their healings. It dawned on me then that chi and this healing spirit were closely related. She was the most faithful person I had ever met. She taught me an important lesson about the value of faith and how you either have it or you don't. I keep her picture on my desk right next to my father's as a reminder of all they taught me.

But it wasn't until my early thirties at the end of an eighteen-month journey around the country with no fixed address that the subject of spirit came up again. I began to feel a longing, a call to spirit. I read many books on the subject trying to satisfy this deep longing that I could not identify precisely.

In my journey around America I visited with a number of lesbian separatists, who had left society as we know it and moved into communes that had no dealings with men. It was here I was introduced to the writings of Ruth and Jean Mountaingrove, a journal called *Sinister Wisdom*, and Starhawk's *The Spiral Dance*. The ideas were a little far-out for me, and I was a little uncomfortable with the notion of a goddess and witches, but something rang true that I could not identify at the time. I was also put off by the separatist idea, as it seemed that since men and women were put here on Earth together we should find a way to get along instead of dropping out to live a life of deprivation and dirt.

In 1978 a friend introduced me to Carl Howie, the senior minister of Westminster Presbyterian Church in Detroit, who now has a center named after him at Union Theological Seminary. I asked him to explain salvation without using the word "saved." The explanations I had heard previously were circular and not very clear. Dr. Howie chose instead to explain the existential plight of mankind and simply said that any church sets itself about answering the questions of why we are here, whether we are we doing the right thing, and what happens to us when we die. His explanation made sense to me, and I agreed to become baptized. But I have to tell you that to this day the notion of Jesus dying for my sins doesn't make a bit of sense to me. I wanted community. My baptism took place at the 11:00 a.m. service with about five hundred people in attendance. I cried through the whole thing and was very moved by the ancient and holy ritual. For the first time in my life I felt like I belonged…well, until the issue of ordaining gay and lesbian clergy came up.

The week after my baptism I attended a regional gathering of women in the church. I spoke up a couple times, and at the social hour I saw a woman coming toward me from across the room like a shark. I don't remember her name, but she asked me if I would like to serve on the Synod Committee on Women. What did I know? I said yes. Evidently the usual route to serving on a regional committee takes years of serving in the trenches at your local church, then on a presbytery committee, and then finally the Synod. Well, I leaped right over all that in one week.

In 1980 I attended a gathering of Presbyterian women in Syracuse, New York. The speakers were Rosemary Reuther, Beverly Harrison, and other famous women theologians of the day. I was quite impressed and very relieved that someone was finally integrating my feminist beliefs and the seemingly contradictory Christian views on women. The seminar with Johanna Bos from Louisville Seminary blew me away. She had translated her own version of the Old Testament and was fond of pointing out how some the translations of the passages involving women were wrong. I loved that woman, sitting there cross-legged on the floor surrounded by handwritten yellow legal pads, in a cloud of cigarette smoke, pontificating in her Dutch accent, "You see how they translated...well, that is just wrong; it should be...." She changed my whole understanding of the Old Testament and women's roles in the Bible.

I started reading everything I could find about feminist theology and women's spirituality as well. Starhawk's *Dreaming the Dark*, written in 1982, and *Truth or Dare* from 1988 changed how I looked at the world forevermore. It moved me from a sense of helplessness to one of personal power to take action, which has stayed with me all these years. Mary Daly's book *Beyond God the Father*, published in 1973, which I did not read until the early eighties started me over the edge, but it was Daly's *Websters' First New Intergalactic Wickedary of the English Language Conjured in Cahoots with Jane Caputi* in which they redefined many words within a lesbian feminist context, that completed the job. I had never thought about how important language was and how redefining the language in that way changed how you think.

In 1988, I moved to the Washington, DC, area and found the Silver Spring Presbyterian Church and its pastor, Margee Iddings. She was, for me, the Syracuse gathering and everything I had read all rolled into one. Coincidentally, upon my arrival several crises arose in the congregation. It came to light that the previous pastor had had inappropriate sexual relations with several members of the church, and termites destroyed the sanctuary (unrelated, most likely, but you never know about these things). I was impressed with how Margee handled both of these situations. But what really impressed me was her preaching. She did not preach the dogma of the mainstream Christian churches. She preached feminist theology peppered with a good dose of humanitarian common sense, and it became quite clear that she had read all the same books I had. We became good friends, and when she left the church to open a retreat in Western Maryland I followed her. Her departure made it clear that I had been attending the Church of Margee and not the Presbyterian Church at all.

Just before we left, there were two defining moments that reinforced my departure. One took place at a meeting of the Session (the governing body of the local church). Charles, a wonderful gay man and self-professed pagan, applied for membership to the church. One of the Session members, a tight-assed lawyer "and son of a missionary," said Charles could not become a member of our church.

I asked, "Why not?"

He said, "Charles has to profess that Jesus is his lord and savior."

I said, "He is willing to do that, but where is it written that you have to profess that Jesus is your ONLY lord and savior?"

The lawyer turned apoplectic, red in the face, and could only sputter. It dawned on me at that moment that this was where the Christian religion goes wrong. The minute you choose between me and you, you're screwed. Jesus had no restrictions, no requirements, no choosing between who is included and who isn't. What part of "love your neighbor" is this policy based on? Once you choose between who can join and who can't, it is a short slippery slope to choosing who leads…as in straight white males, for instance. No gay men, lesbians, or women need apply. No persons of color either while we are at it. Pffffft! What nonsense!

About this same time I attended the General Assembly of the Presbyterian Church USA. The issue of ordaining gay and lesbian clergy was voted on and turned down as it had been many times before. The PLGC, the gay and lesbian Presbyterian organization, organized a demonstration protesting the vote. We were to solemnly and silently march down the center aisle carrying signs and a cross. All very gay-boy melodramatic, someone pounded a nail or two in the cross up at the front. I was holding one end of a large banner, and the other end was held by a man dressed in a leather S&M outfit. I noticed that several members of my church, led by Margee, were getting up and join-ing the procession. They squeezed in beside me, and I started to cry. These people loved me, and for the first time straight people were standing up for me.

But as I stood there looking out over the audience of plain, ordinary, middle-class, educated fellow Americans who had just rejected my lifestyle and reinforced all the nonsense spewed by the Religion Right about homosexuality, an enormous epiphany dawned on me. Why was I choosing to be part of this hypocrisy? These good, decent, orderly folk out there in the audience had just spit in my face. It couldn't have been clearer if they had called me a bull-dagger dyke. That was it! I never went back to church.

This brings us to 1992, the beginning of several years designed to test my spirit. In May 1992 my partner of thirteen years and I broke up, and in November my father died. The breakup had been in the making for three years, and it finally came to a head. There wasn't a lot of drama surrounding it, but there sure was a lot of pain.

I had not been particularly close to my father at this point. My mother had died ten years earlier, and I did not stay in close contact with him after her death. I called once or twice a year and had not visited him for years. During a brief visit in the summer of 1992 at his house in Volcano, on the Big Island of Hawaii, I let myself believe that he was doing OK and flew home after a few days. I had arranged for a friend to clean for him. She called me the next day and demanded to know what the hell I was thinking. She said (yelled) that my father was in bad shape even if I did not let myself see it and I needed to get back to Volcano to take care of him. I agonized about it for a day or two and finally decided that she was right. Back I went.

Even after spending $1,080 to fly back, I was still unsure of what to do—whether I should stay, put him in a care facility (which he begged me not to do), or just go home and forget about the whole thing, something I had done successfully for years. I could not decide. A friend suggested going to see a famous psychic surgeon who was coming to Kona. I had never heard of a psychic surgeon, but I went. I lay down on the table, and it seemed to me that he actually put his hand in my abdomen and drew something out. I know this is really hard to believe, but that is what it looked like. Afterward I had red marks but no bruises. When he finished it was clear as a bell that I needed to stay and take care of my father.

We fixed up my father's house, bought him a new La-Z-Boy, and settled in. I took advantage of the new Family Medical Leave

Act (which I had lobbied Congress to get passed) and stayed twelve weeks. I am so glad I did. He and I both knew he was going to die. He refused to go to dialysis even though he was living on 10 percent of his kidney function. He stopped taking his insulin and blood pressure medicine and lived quite well for four months. He slept a lot but was not in pain and did not seem to be suffering at all. But most importantly we talked and talked.

Spending that time with him was an amazing gift. He was a very intelligent man, very well-read, but an emotional adolescent. I think he finally grew up during those last few weeks. He took stock of his life, and I think he judged himself fairly. He talked about where he thought he had succeeded and failed as a father and husband. He talked about his career as an oceanographer, telling me about his adventures in the Arctic, the Antarctic with Admiral Perry, developing sonar during World War II, and being at the Bikini Atoll when they set off the A-bomb. He talked about my mother and how much he loved her. He had verbally and psychologically abused her for years, yet he talked about how much he loved her. It was very strange that he seemed totally unaware of the abuse. But all in all, it was a rare honor to be there for the final reckoning of a remarkable life.

I returned home to DC with no idea of how my life was going to change. I decided to join the Mintwood Zendo. There I was exposed to the teachings of Bobby Rhodes (Soeng Hyang) from the Providence Zen Center, Rhode Island. She came to DC to do a series of weekend retreats. By this time I was forty-seven years old. I went on retreat, and while in a session with her, I had an enlightened experience during which I encountered a profound connection to the universe. We had been talking about a koan, a Zen teaching tool where they give you a riddle to solve, and suddenly I got it. I saw in a deep, mystical way how we are all connected from the beginning of time to the end of time, in every direction—every person, animal, plant, and mineral. That realization continues to reside deep in me.

In 1994 I started taking classes in Re-evaluation Counseling. On the surface it seems to be a peer counseling technique, but at the deeper levels it is clear that the founder, Harvey Jackins, was influenced by the Buddhists. RC preaches the same wisdom of returning to the present moment (impermanence) and not imposing judgment on things as they happen (equanimity) as the Buddhists.

Finally, in 1997, I was given the opportunity to make sense of all that had happened to me before that moment when the blood vessel burst. I am grateful that I had a Buddhist practice. I once attended a gathering of women Presbyterian ministers at Rising Phoenix, Margee Iddings' retreat site. I was the massage therapist there, and they invited me to join them to talk about their understanding of God. They went around the circle saying things like, "I am made in God's image," or "I believe in the 'indwelling God.'" When it was my turn I said, "There is no separation between me and the divine; I am not an image; there is no separate being that dwells within me. I am 'God,' as are the chairs in this room and the air and the trees and birds outside the window. At the quantum level there is no difference between us at all. I do not believe there is a God to punish me for some transgression or a God to test my faith like Job—nor do I believe a God will save me from my suffering. I am sure it is up to me. I will be happy if I trust in the inherent goodness of the world and the connectedness of all beings."

It is up to me to choose to suffer or not. It is up to me to be cheerful or grumpy. I believe the world is a benevolent place. I believe in the Buddhist teachings of impermanence and equanimity: everything changes and nothing has any inherent value. We get to assign value to it. If we cling to the idea of wanting things to stay the same we will suffer.

I have taken a vow to follow the Five Mindfulness Trainings taught by Thich Nhat Hanh. Briefly, they are that I promise not to kill, harm, exploit, steal from, or oppress any people, animals, plants, or minerals. I promise to behave in a sexually responsible manner. I promise to practice mindful speech, to speak truthfully, with words that inspire self-confidence with everyone I talk to. Finally, I promise to cultivate good health for me and everyone else on the planet by mindful consumption and not to consume more than I need. I take these promises very seriously. (See Appendix 1 for the full text.)

These promises inspire a sense of integrity in me. I know who I am. I am not searching for who I am anymore. The crucible of age, events, and faith in the goodness of life has forged a solid core. I believe I could, like Sir Thomas More, survive a king's demand that I change my mind. I believe I could be as strong as Joan of Arc, Gandhi, or Nelson Mandela.

A few years ago the LGBT community center fell apart. I was the Chair of the Board. We were suddenly seriously in debt for failing to supervise the Executive Director properly. Several Board members, my best friend among them, resigned. I was incredulous! It was our duty, as the governing body that hired this man and then failed to supervise him, to rectify the situation, not walk away from it. One Board member and I stuck it out and with the help of a few others raised enough money to put the center back in the black. There were a few sleepless nights, some serious worry, but in the end we prevailed. I don't think I could have lived with myself if I had walked away.

Everything I have experienced in my life has brought me to this point—all the good things I did and all the stupid things I did. If I had been born in a different time to a different family, chosen different partners to spend my life with, I would be a different person. I am instead one who, as my friend Brigitte is fond of saying, dashes into the middle of something, shakes the tree, and then is incredulous that the apples come bouncing down on my head. I know that I am a hand stirring the water in a bucket, and when I am gone the water will return to what it was doing before I arrived. But while I am stirring the water it is important to me that I do it mindfully, decently, and in order, with a loving heart, never forgetting how we are all connected.

Chapter 17

Me and the Homeless

I was riding in my scooter down Seventeenth Street in Washington, DC, one day with a friend when we encountered William on the corner of Seventeenth and N. This was his usual hangout. William was a schizophrenic who had been released from the mental hospital under the Early Release Program started by President Ronald Reagan. Most days he was present and friendly. Some days, though, his demons put him through his paces. But this day he was exuberantly present. Upon seeing me he jumped down off the brick wall he was sitting on and gave me a big hug.

My friend was horrified, and after we left him she asked why in the world I had hugged this homeless man who probably had lice and who knows what else. I said it was because he and I share a deep spiritual connection. We both have a personal experience with the cosmic joke that you never know how life will turn out. This knowledge keeps us from taking ourselves too seriously and opens us up to embrace everyone else who has suffered like us. It is the Namaste: I acknowledge the divine in you. I honor that he

165

suffers, and he returns the favor. But, I told my friend, you will probably not truly understand this until something happens to you like what has happened to me and to him.

William and I were old friends. I passed by his spot two or three times a week in my scooter, and at some point in the past we had begun a conversation. One day he asked if he could give me a hug, and I said yes. We had good laugh when we both realized that this was the only hug each of us would get this week. Hugs became our usual greeting after that.

William was homeless most of the time. Occasionally he had a job as a bike courier, but mostly he sat on his wall and greeting passersby. He was shabbily dressed, hair coiffed in a wild Afro and run-down shoes on his feet.

A few blocks north of where William sat, Keesha and Shawna were always hanging out in front of the 7-Eleven at the corner of Seventeenth and R Street. Keesha was a teenager who lived with her grandmother nearby, seemingly of very low IQ, and she often had self-inflicted slash wounds on her arms and legs in direct contrast to her usual sunny personality. She was perpetually happy. Shawna, on the other hand, was a skinny, scrawny crack addict in her forties and a grandmother of six. Shawna was a wheeler-dealer and always had a scheme up her sleeve. Her natural state was grumpy, but she could be cajoled into pleasantness easily enough if I stopped and talked with her. These two could be found in front of that store morning, noon, and night. I saw them nearly every day. I gave them some change each every day and twenty dollars on their birthday and on Christmas. Of course, Shawna tried to convince me several times a year that it was her birthday.

My apartment was burgled once, and I approached the girls to find out if they knew who did it.

"What'd they take?" they asked

"A TV, a computer, and all my earrings," I said.

They said they had seen someone trying to sell a TV and computer earlier that day.

"Let's go to the police," I said.

"Oh no," they said. "We don't do police."

"Well, then," I said. "Could you make their lives miserable for me?

"Oh yes!" they said enthusiastically. "Uh huh! We can do that!"

So off they went to spread a little misery and left me feeling good that justice had been served.

One October Keesha was looking very shabby. She normally was well-kept, but she was dirty and had clearly been wearing her clothes for days. She also had fresh cuts on her arm. I asked what happened, and she told me her grandmother had died and she had been evicted from the apartment because her name was not on the lease. I thought to myself that she would never survive the winter on the street. I contacted a social worker friend and asked what could be done. Nothing, it seemed, except to get her into a homeless shelter. But I knew that the shelters turned everyone out during the day and would only let them stay there at night. I didn't think she could handle that.

"Can we get her into some sort of residential program?" I asked.

The only program that had space was an alcohol treatment program.

"Does she have an alcohol problem?" my friend asked.

"She does now," I said.

So I went to the 7-Eleven, took Keesha into the store, and bought a beer.

"Drink this," I said.

"I don't like beer," she said.

"But," I said, "You have to appear to have a drinking problem in order to get in this program. So when the social worker asks you, you say you get drunk every day."

"OK," she said. We went to meet the social worker. She was accepted and spent the winter safe and sound in the residential program. I only saw her once more in the spring. She had gained about forty pounds—liked the food there, she said. And she liked too that they sat around mornings and afternoons talking in a group. She disappeared after that, during the winter, and I never saw her again. I heard from the Ethiopians who ran the 7-Eleven that she had gone south to be with her family.

Veronica, when I first met her, was the cleaning woman at the Maunter Project. She was always cheerful and did a great job of cleaning the office. I was in need of someone to clean for me, especially to do my laundry. I had just returned home from living with friends after I got out of the rehab hospital. I could not manage the steps to the basement where the laundry was located. I hired Veronica to clean for me once a month.

The first day she was to arrive, I got a phone call from a store some blocks from my house. Veronica was there and needed directions, they said. I gave them the directions to my house. A few minutes later I received another phone call. Veronica is here and needs directions, they said. I smiled and gave the directions. A few minutes later I received another phone call. Veronica is here and needs directions, they said. *Oh my,* I thought to myself, *this is getting to be a problem*. But the last call was from the 7-Eleven half a block away. She finally arrived at my door. We repeated this scene for six months until she finally figured out how to get to my house.

She told me she had been raised in the Maryland Children's Home after her mother abandoned her and her sister. They told her she was retarded. I didn't think she was, because she could manage everything but geographic directions. I think she was learning disabled. But never mind; this has nothing much to do with the story.

I looked forward to the day she came over to clean. She left my apartment sparkling, my laundry neatly folded and put away in the right places. I would hang around until she arrived so we could have breakfast together. She had a very different way of cooking eggs than I was used to, and I liked them a lot. She would fry the eggs, poke the yolks, cover the eggs with a lot of salt and pepper and cook them until they were hard. Doesn't sound like something that would be as good as it tasted. We had many discussions over breakfast and sometimes over dinner if she was still there when I got home. Once we went out to dinner at the Italian Kitchen, and I told her she could have a drink if she wanted. She got into a discussion with the waiter about a particular drink she had had there before. He could not figure out what she meant, so she went over to the bar and gave instructions. She had a glowing personality that served her well.

She was in her late forties and was experiencing the symptoms of menopause. She brought it up because she thought she was getting sick with the hot flashes. She had never known anyone who had gone through "the change" and had no idea what was happening to her. She was raised in an institution. Amazing what you miss.

After a year or so I started seeing someone in Baltimore and was often gone for the weekend. I arranged for Veronica to come on Fridays and invited her to stay over to Monday. She loved staying at my place. She lived in the projects in Section 8 housing and didn't like the noise there. She got to be well-known about Dupont Circle, where I lived. Don't ask me how, but she became tight with the drag queens that hung out at a bar nearby.

I have always been a generous person, but living my life from the wheelchair has given me a new perspective. I receive very little money to live on. I understand now that I am simply a steward of this money. It is not my money; it never was my money, even when I was earning more than double what I get today. It is also very clear to me that you reap what you sow. I made a conscious decision to give money to the homeless on the street for years and gave a little to everyone who asked. And when I needed money in the rehab hospital my friends gave me thirteen thousand dollars. There is an ebb and flow to money in my life, and I trust the universe now to provide what I need. But I don't just sit here and wait for it to arrive. I advertise, and I apply for jobs. And I am grateful when money comes my way to pay the rent or buy a ticket to a concert.

No one tells me how to spend my money, and I don't tell the homeless who beg from me how to spend their money. They can make a decision to buy something to eat or to buy drugs. It's their decision. I wish the agencies that control my life had the same attitude. Instead I am made to jump through humiliating hoop after hoop, treated as though I were a child instead of an adult. I don't like it and will not pass it down the line to the homeless I meet on the street. If you truly believe that we are all made in the Christian god's image, or believe in Buddha's teaching that one way of life is not particularly better than another, I encourage you to give money to the homeless with a smile in your heart.

Chapter 18

Grace, Gratitude, and No Regrets

"Wake up!" Buddhist teacher Bobbie Rhodes said to me once, clapping her hands once very loudly in my face. "Wake up! It is all waiting for you if you just open your eyes." So I did! I woke up to how keenly aware I am of how we are all connected and to the abundance of the universe. There is a magnificent abundance out there if we just pay attention.

At meals I give thanks to each person who had a part in setting this food in front of me. It includes the people who prepared it, who sold it in the store, who transported it, who harvested it, who planted it and maintained it. Thanks too to the people who provided the water, the land, and grew the seeds. And then I could on a good day also include all the people who built the trucks and the buildings, who mined the minerals and cut the wood and who grew the trees, until I realize that nearly everyone in the world has something to do with putting this food in front of me. It is true about everything you see in front of you: your clothes, your furniture, your electronics, and the paint on your wall. Think about it. Everything you use has a long history and literally millions of people involved in its life. I breathe in immense gratitude for being so connected.

I started a genealogical project last year to locate every relative I could. I started with eight known people and wound up with 135 people on my family tree. Once I had exhausted the ancients I started looking for living relatives and located my second cousin, Hardy Spoehr, who was by some miracle living just down the street. He was as excited as I was to locate another relative.

I had a dream years ago about my Apache grandmother, Georgia Coleson, standing in front of an assembly hall that looked like the United Nations. In the first row were people I knew, like my mother and father; in the row behind them were relatives whose names I knew but had never met. Behind them were thousands of rows of my ancestors. My grandmother shook her finger at me, saying, "Margaret, you always forget; you are not alone, and you always forget." I am not alone. I am grateful for the connections living and dead, grateful for the thousand bits of DNA that have been passed down to me.

I am grateful to that benign little blood vessel that burst in my spinal cord. No malice, no forethought, not evil, just a little blood vessel with a weak wall. I can't say that I might feel differently about this if someone had deliberately injured me or if I had done something to injure myself. I might, but that is not my story.

That little blood vessel has provided a richness to my life that I am not sure I ever would have attained on my own. I now experience moments of grace every day.

Most moments are little moments of grace, not big epiphanies. They are the little things: a beautiful sunset, a child's delight at a smile from you, the excitement of making a new friend, or a hug from an old friend you haven't seen in a while. They put their arms around you, and the whole universe falls into place. Most of us don't notice these moments of grace. We get in our cars, turn on the radios, rush to the stores where music plays overhead, dash in, buy something, dash out, zoom off to the next place, all the while with cell phones stuck in our ear. When we are graceless, we are rude to clerks, make obscene gestures to people in traffic, yell a little too loudly to our children to shut up, or forget to kiss our spouses goodnight. We wander about with our heads up our asses, totally engrossed with what is happening inside our heads or on the cell phone. A friend shared with me once about how much she liked smoking marijuana because it made all the colors brighter, the sounds sweeter, and the air fresher. Wake up! You can experience this on a daily basis without a drug, as I do. It's there waiting for you to notice.

As I made my way through the rehab hospital and tried to reestablish a life for myself, I had many doubts. At times it was overwhelming. I went on retreat and burned off my anger, but still so much of life was uncertain. I felt isolated. For a while I felt abandoned by friends and whatever my concept of the divine was. How do you reconcile these things? How do you make sense of random accidents? I had attended the Mintwood Zendo, but I was not skilled in meditation nor very well versed in Buddhist teachings at the time.

Why did this happen to me? This is one question I can assure you with great confidence has no answer. Shit happens, and you deal with it. There is no why or wherefore. Things happen, and you get to decide what they mean. You get to decide whether to suffer or not. You get to decide whether the journey will be miserable or the most fascinating ride you have ever taken. If you can find a way to plug in, you will thrive. It matters little whether that plug is Buddha, Jesus, Mohammad, Judaism, Hinduism, Khalil Gibran, Joseph Smith, Mary Baker Eddy, or if you just figure out something else for yourself. We are all part of something bigger, and we are all connected to each other in wondrous ways, no matter what you call it.

A friend of mine is a sixty-eight-year-old African-American woman born in rural Kentucky, the ninth of ten children, raised very poor and often without enough to eat. She was the first Black student to integrate her school and took a lot of abuse for it. But she has done very well with her life, got two degrees, and raised a child. We were talking about self-esteem one day. We were sitting close to each other, and I looked her in the eye and told her she was "good, totally good, without exception." I repeated this several times, and as she took it in she began to cry.

After a few minutes of this, she sat back and said, "Wait. I need to take a breath and wrap my head around this. After the way I was raised, here I am living in beautiful Hawaii, and after all I suffered as a black woman, this white woman is sitting here telling me I am good." Needless to say, we both were crying by this point. If I never accomplish another thing before I die, I know I have done something right if by my efforts just one woman of color hears that she is treasured, respected, honored… and good. This was a big moment of grace for the two of us. You can have these moments if you set aside all the grasping at a racial identity, or wondering if someone will like you or not, or worrying that you are exposing yourself somehow.

I love all the little ironies of life. I love the unexpected surprises. I jiggle my world to make sure it goes my way. A woman in my building who has an electric scooter like mine asked me one day if I thought people were rude to me because I'm in a wheelchair. I said, "Never; people are kind and friendly and cheerful toward me." As we parted she headed off toward a bus stop filled with people. She rang her bicycle bell loudly, yelling for people to get out of her way. I had to laugh. Who exactly was being rude and unfriendly? She was a glum person with a perpetual frown, and she complained in every encounter I had with her. You reap what you sow. She created a world around her that reinforced her perception of the world. I think the world is a nice place, and I smile at almost everyone I meet out on the sidewalk. They smile back. What a great thing.

Not long after I was disabled I was lamenting that I was no longer contributing to society. A friend sitting with me said, "Well that is because you have never accompanied yourself in a roll down the street." I said, "What do you mean?" She said, "You sprinkle fairy dust all along the way. You greet everyone on the street with a smile, you cheerfully give money every day to the homeless women in front of the 7-Eleven, you wave at the crossing guard, and you get into a conversation with every clerk who waits on you." I was flabbergasted. "I don't do that!" I protested. "I am no Pollyanna." "No, not Pollyanna," she said, "just someone who enjoys life and shows it, just like those goofy little monks who visit from Tibet who find everything wonderful and funny."

Once I was crossing the street, and an older woman in a car did not see me in the crosswalk. She slammed on her brakes at the last possible moment. As I caught my breath I looked up at her just as she did the same. As we caught each other's eyes we burst out laughing in a delicious moment of grace. She was thankful that she had not run over me. I was thankful that she had not run over me, and we shared that moment of gratitude. In a different moment, I could have been angry and yelled at her, but I like this way better.

I do find most of life very funny. It is really quite hilarious out there. Another day when I was in the crosswalk, a woman kept coming at me, clearly not seeing me, giving me quite a fright. I got her attention by shouting obscenities at her. I made it over to the curb and burst out laughing at myself. I imagine myself to be this calm, peaceful Buddhist, yet here I was yelling at this woman who scared me.

Children get it. They understand grace until it is stamped out of them. A little boy was looking at me the other day by bending over and looking at me through his legs. Another talking to me on the bus said with a serious little face that he was asking for a scooter like mine for Christmas. Made my heart smile. Two little girls who used to visit me played a game where we each threw a deck of cards into the air and shrieked. It was great fun.

The flip side of grace is regret. Regret can be an evil snake that slithers in. I wish I had done…. I wish hadn't done…. If only I had done things differently. I asked my mother once if she had to do things over what she would have done differently with her life. At first she wrote what she thought I wanted to hear about how she enjoyed being my mother, but on page two she started to wax eloquently about all she had given up and all the things she sacrificed. Six pages later, she stopped. Her life was filled with regret. She attempted suicide twice and finally died at the age of sixty-nine, literally of a broken heart. She never found a way to forgive herself for her decisions. But the truth is that we all do what we can at that moment, whatever the curious intersection of circumstances leads us to. If we could make different decisions we would. I learned this from Byron Katie's books and videos.

Years ago I helped a friend transcribe tapes she had made of older women talking about their lives. I recall one woman reminiscing about teaching kindergarten for one year before she was married forty years ago. That was her main memory of what she had enjoyed the most in life. Yikes! Where had she been for the past forty years?

We are gifted twenty-four hours a day, 365 days a year to pay attention to what is going on around us. Unplug the TV, leave the car radio off, turn off your cell phone (they will leave a message), take the headphones off, cancel the newspaper, and stop watching the news. Subscribe instead to a daily good news webcast, one that sends you pithy sayings every day (such as www.belief.net), and put a nice picture up on your desktop so every time you open your computer it pleases you. Get a book on feng shui, and rearrange your house harmonically. Wake up! Wake up! You have nothing to lose but your illusions.

Five Mindfulness Trainings

The First Mindfulness Training

Aware of the suffering caused by the destruction of life, I am committed to cultivating compassion and learning ways to protect the lives of people, animals, plants, and minerals. I am determined not to kill, not to let others kill, and not to support any act of killing in the world, in my thinking, and in my way of life.

The Second Mindfulness Training

Aware of suffering caused by exploitation, social injustice, stealing, and oppression, I am committed to cultivating loving kindness and learning ways to work for the well-being of people, animals, plants, and minerals. I will practice generosity by sharing my time, energy, and material resources with those who are in real need. I am determined not to steal and not to possess anything that should belong to others. I will respect the property of others, but I will prevent others from profiting from human suffering or the suffering of other species on Earth.

The Third Mindfulness Training

Aware of suffering caused by sexual misconduct, I am committed to cultivating responsibility and learning ways to protect the safety and integrity of individuals, couples, families, and society. I am determined not to engage in sexual relations without love and a long-term commitment. To preserve the happiness of myself and others, I am determined to respect my commitments and the commitments of others. I will do everything in my power to protect children from sexual abuse and to prevent couples and families from being broken by sexual misconduct.

The Fourth Mindfulness Training

Aware of suffering caused by unmindful speech and the inability to listen to others, I am committed to cultivating loving speech and deep listening in order to bring joy and happiness to others and relieve others of their suffering. Knowing that words can create happiness or suffering, I am determined to speak truthfully, with words that inspire self-confidence, joy, and hope. I will not spread news that I do not know to be certain and will not criticize or condemn things of which I am not sure. I will refrain from uttering words that can cause division or discord or that can cause the family or the community to break. I am determined to make all efforts to reconcile all conflicts, however small.

The Fifth Mindfulness Training

Aware of the suffering caused by unmindful consumption, I am committed to cultivating good health, both physical and mental, for myself, my family, and my society by practicing mindful eating, drinking, and consuming. I will ingest only items that preserve peace, well-being, and joy in my body, in my consciousness, and in the collective body and consciousness of my family and society. I am determined not to use alcohol or any other intoxicant or to ingest foods or other items that contain toxins, such as certain TV programs, magazines, books, films, and conversations. I am aware that to damage my body or my consciousness with these poisons is to betray my ancestors, my parents, my society, and future generations. I will work to transform violence, fear, anger, and confusion in myself and in society by practicing a diet for myself and for society. I understand that a proper diet is crucial for self-transformation and for the transformation of society.

Resources

This is list of spinal cord injury organizations and three general disability organizations. It is not a comprehensive list. Check the resource lists on the organization websites.

American Association of People with Disabilities
1629 K Street NW, Suite 950
Washington, DC 20006
http://www.aapd.org
800-840-8844 (Toll Free V/TTY)

National Council on Independent Living
1710 Rhode Island Ave NW, 5th Floor
Washington, DC, 20036
http://www.ncil.org
Toll free 877-525-3400

National Organization on Disability
5 East 86th Street

New York, NY 10028

http://www.nod.org

646-505-1191

National Spinal Cord Injury Association

1 Church Street #600

Rockville, MD 20850

http://www.spinalcord.org/

Toll-free Helpline (800) 962-9629

E-mail: ResourceCenter: info@spinalcord.org

Paralyzed Veterans Association

801 Eighteenth Street, NW

Washington, DC, 20006-3517

http://www.pva.org

800-424-8200

Healthcare hotline 800-232-1782

E-mail: info@pva.org

United Spinal Association

75-20 Astoria Blvd, Suite 120

Jackson Heights, NY 11370

http://www.unitedspinal.org/

Toll free 800-404-2898

E-mail: info@unitedspinal.org

Appendix III

Miscellaneous References

Access Surf Hawaii
P.O. Box 15152
Honolulu, HI 96830
http://www.accesssurf.org
808-236-4200

Belief Net
http://www.belief.net

New Mobility Magazine (I think this is the best magazine in the world)
http://www.newmobility.com

The Re-evaluation Counseling Communities
719 Second Avenue North
Seattle, WA 98109
http://www.rc.org

Phone 206-284-0311

E-mail: ircc@rc.og

Sounds True, Inc

413 S. Arthur Street

Louisville, CO 80027

http://www.soundstrue.com

800-333-9185

E-mail: customerservice@soundstrue.com

Made in the USA
Charleston, SC
06 March 2014